D1796402

Poland

Decentralization and Reform of the State

246146

The World Bank
Washington, D.C.

377300

Copyright © 1992
The International Bank for Reconstruction
and Development/THE WORLD BANK
1818 H Street, N.W.
Washington, D.C. 20433, U.S.A.

World Bank Country Studies are among the many reports originally prepared for internal use as part of the continuing analysis by the Bank of the economic and related conditions of its developing member countries and of its dialogues with the governments. Some of the reports are published in this series with the least possible delay for the use of governments and the academic, business and financial, and development communities. The typescript of this paper therefore has not been prepared in accordance with the procedures appropriate to formal printed texts, and the World Bank accepts no responsibility for errors.

The World Bank does not guarantee the accuracy of the data included in this publication and accepts no responsibility whatsoever for any consequence of their use. Any maps that accompany the text have been prepared solely for the convenience of readers; the designations and presentation of material in them do not imply the expression of any opinion whatsoever on the part of the World Bank, its affiliates, or its Board or member countries concerning the legal status of any country, territory, city, or area or of the authorities thereof or concerning the delimitation of its boundaries or its national affiliation.

The material in this publication is copyrighted. Requests for permission to reproduce portions of it should be sent to the Office of the Publisher at the address shown in the copyright notice above. The World Bank encourages dissemination of its work and will normally give permission promptly and, when the reproduction is for noncommercial purposes, without asking a fee. Permission to copy portions for classroom use is granted through the Copyright Clearance Center, 27 Congress Street, Salem, Massachusetts 01970, U.S.A.

The complete backlist of publications from the World Bank is shown in the annual *Index of Publications*, which contains an alphabetical title list (with full ordering information) and indexes of subjects, authors, and countries and regions. The latest edition is available free of charge from the Distribution Unit, Office of the Publisher, Department F, The World Bank, 1818 H Street, N.W., Washington, D.C. 20433, U.S.A., or from Publications, The World Bank, 66, avenue d'Iéna, 75116 Paris, France.

ISSN: 0253-2123

Library of Congress Cataloging-in-Publication Data

Poland : decentralization and reform of the state.
    p.   cm. — (A World Bank country study)
  " This report reflects findings of a mission that visited Poland in
1991"—CIP preface.
  ISBN 0-8213-2213-3
    1. Poland—Economic policy—1981–   2. Decentralization in
government—Poland. 3. Local finance—Poland.   I. Series.
HC340.3.P6435   1992
338.9438—dc20   92-23415
                                            CIP

PREFACE

This report reflects the findings of a mission that visited Poland during December 1991. This main mission was comprised of Messrs. J. Hicks (mission leader), R. Carrier, L. Ficinski-Dunin, J. Norregaard, and R. Prud'homme.

The mission would like to thank the Central Government authorities of several ministries that provided support to the mission, and in particular, the Office for Local Government, Council of Ministers, for facilitating the mission's visits to local governments. The mission visited (during two missions in 1991) the following local governments: Garwolin, Katowice, Kielce, Krakow, Jablonna, Lublin, Lubomia, Radom, Siewearz, Szudlowiec, Warsaw, and Zabrze. The hospitality and collaboration of officials of these gminas, as well as those of their respective Voivodships, are gratefully acknowledged; without their support, this report would not have been possible.

The main report (Chapters I-VII) was written by James Hicks. The main report is based on contributions by mission members, as presented in Annexes I-VIII. John Norregaard (OECD) provided inputs to the normative framework of the main report (Chapter II).

The Annexes provide detailed findings of the missions that visited Poland in June and December 1991. It should be noted that these Annexes reflect the situation in late 1991 and that they provide data collected from different sources that are not always compatible. Therefore, there may be mistakes of data and/or their interpretation. Despite these possible drawbacks, however, these Annexes present a rather comprehensive overview of Poland's local public sector assembled in one document. It is hoped that this will be useful for policy makers and analysts that must go beyond the broad design of reform policy and examine details of how to make the reforming system work better.

The Annexes were prepared under the supervision of J. Hicks. The primary authors of each Annex are: B. Kaminski for Annexes I, III, and IV; R. Prud'homme, Annex II; R. Carrier (with support from L. Ficinski), Annexes V, VI (Section C), VII and VIII; and J. Cracknell (supported by L. Ficinski), Annex VI.

Department Director	Mr. Kemal Dervis
Lead Economist	Mr. Ulrich Thumm
Division Chief	Mr. Hans Apitz
Peer Reviewer	Mr. David Vetter

Currency Equivalents

Currency Unit = Zloty (Zl)

Calendar 1991 US$1 = 10,559 Zlotys (Average)
January 31, 1992 US$1 = 11,483 Zlotys

Polish Fiscal Year

January 1 to December 31

Glossary of Abbreviations and Polish Terms

CEM	Country Economic Memorandum of the World Bank, "Poland: Economic Transformation at a Crossroads", February 5, 1992 (Green Cover)
ETP	Economic Transformation Program
FAIP	Financial Action and Investment Plan
GDP	Gross Domestic Product
Gmina	Polish Local Government (municipality)
LSGA	Local Self-Government Act of March 22, 1990
MDA	Municipal Development Agency
OECD	Organisation for Economic Co-Operation and Development
Voivodship	Administrative Region of Polish Central Government

Weights and Measures = Metric System

TABLE OF CONTENTS

CHAPTER I. ECONOMIC TRANSFORMATION AT A CROSSROADS: ROLE OF LOCAL GOVERNMENTS

1.   Poland's sweeping reform package, the Economic Transformation Program (ETP), is now at a crossroads. Launched in January 1990, the ETP has been successful in many areas, but so far it has failed to deliver growth; GDP fell by about 12 percent in 1990 and about 8 percent in 1991. Furthermore, the clear danger of sliding back into hyperinflation leaves little choice but fiscal retrenchment for 1992 and perhaps beyond.[1]

2.   Decentralization is an important part of Poland's democratization drive and of the Government's economic transition program. The fundamental break, from the state as implementation agent of the central plan, to a decentralized state with autonomous local governments accountable to their constituents, began with passage of the Local Self-Government Act (LSGA) in March 1990. This represents a significant part of the reform of economic and political relationships between the Polish state and its citizens.

3.   Decentralization may provide significant benefits. Among these are improved accountability of public officials to their constituents and economic efficiency gains resulting from local governments providing and financing infrastructure and services that are clearly local in impact.

4.   Decentralization also presents significant risks. In Poland's current situation, the primary risk is local government behavior that could lead to excessive and unpredictable demands on the central budget, contributing to fiscal deficits that promote runaway inflation. As Poland's democratic process continues, this risk will become greater if mayors may appeal successfully to Ministers and/or Members of Parliament of the same political party for ever-increasing fiscal transfers to finance local projects. Local politicians around the world always prefer a "we spend but they pay" environment that minimizes the political cost of local beneficiaries paying for local services, but this opens a "black hole" in the central budget, with recourse to inflationary financing in which all citizens lose. To avoid this, it is urgent that Poland develop clear and reasonable decentralization "rules of the game" so that (a) partisan politics are minimized in intergovernmental affairs and (b) both national and local politicians are held accountable for the responsibilities assigned to each.

5.   The primary objective of this report is to take stock of Poland's progress in decentralization to local governments within the context of the Government's transition program, and to make recommendations on how decentralization policy may support, broaden and deepen transition objectives. The transition program is at a crossroads, however, and making decentralization of the state consistent with the short and medium-term stabilization and growth objectives of this program requires clear decisions about the pace and scope of decentralization. Therefore, the analysis and

---

[1]/ See The World Bank's Country Economic Memorandum (CEM), "Poland: Economic Transformation at a Crossroads", Report No. 10305-POL, May 29, 1992. Henceforth cited as CEM.

specific recommendations of the chapters to come are guided by the following parameters required for consistency with the Government's transition program:

(a)   the fiscal demands of local governments on the central budget should be the minimum amount consistent with local government responsibilities and own-source resource mobilization potential; and

(b)   decentralization of public sector responsibilities to local governments should generate as little disruption and confusion as possible so that key national officials do not divert unnecessarily their attention from urgent, macroeconomic demands of the transition program.

6.   The stakes of successful decentralization are high. Currently, local government expenditures represent about 11 percent of general government expenditures, and 4 percent of GDP. About one-half of these expenditures are financed with central government taxes shared with or transferred to local governments; this accounts for approximately eight percent of central budget expenditures.

7.   The decentralization program may contribute effectively to both the short- and medium-term strategies recommended in the CEM. In facing the immediate danger of runaway inflation, resulting from monetization of a potential fiscal deficit of 10 percent of GDP or higher in 1992, an effective decentralization strategy may reduce the demand on the central budget by about one-half of the 1991 level of fiscal transfers, or one percent of GDP (Chapter IV). This may be achieved through improved cost recovery from local beneficiaries and enhanced local tax mobilization. This represents the same order of magnitude noted in the CEM (para. 45) for possible budgetary savings that could result from postponement of wage increases, curtailment of housing finance subsidies, and a temporary drop in investments. Furthermore, effective linking of decentralization with reform of the financial sector may support the medium-term strategy for stability and growth. In particular, the decentralization strategy should include substitution of fiscal resources for financing local government investments with prudent borrowing on competitive market terms from domestic capital markets (Chapter V).

8.   Local government expenditures will tend to be an increasing share of general government expenditures as decentralization proceeds. Furthermore, it is likely that a second tier of local government will be created in the future, and this would mean that an even larger proportion of public sector expenditures would be sub-national, especially in the infrastructure area where local governments could account for well over one-half of total infrastructure investments. Thus, current decentralization decisions will influence the more substantial decentralization actions of the future. It is important that current decisions establish the correct precedents regarding, for example, local resource mobilization, accountability and investment financing, so that Poland may avoid mistakes made in other countries (e.g., Argentina, Brazil) about central/local relations that have contributed to disastrous results of macroeconomic destabilization that ultimately hurt most the poor.

9.   Within this context, and for reasons elaborated later in this report, the top priorities for Government action to promote decentralization and reform of the state as part of the transition program are the following:

(a)   designate or create an institution with the overall responsibility for formulation and implementation of decentralization policy;

(b)   keep the decentralization agenda as simple as possible; local governments should concentrate on infrastructure and services that are clearly local in impact and for which they may be held clearly accountable by local citizens; if significant ambiguities exist regarding assignment of a service to the central or local governments, keep the service centralized in the short-term;

(c)   eliminate central controls and constraints on activities considered to be under local responsibility (e.g., caps on public housing rents and property tax rates) and promote direct cost recovery from direct beneficiaries of local services; promote local resource mobilization through clear assignment of responsibilities and clearly limited and predictable fiscal transfers; taxes (first local and then national) should be considered the financing source of last resort for local infrastructure and services; the substitution of national fiscal revenues currently shared or transferred to local governments with local user charges would represent a reduction of demand on the state budget of approximately one percent of GDP; enhanced local tax mobilization could reduce this demand even further;

(d)   discourage or reject (i) municipally owned or controlled banks that are not fully subject to market discipline and prudential regulation and (ii) municipal ownership and operation of enterprises of a commercial nature that should be privatized, and do not establish subsidized lines of credit for local governments or their enterprises; and

(e)   delay the decision about creation of a second tier of local government until the current municipal tier is performing adequately and the crossroads stage of the economic transition program has passed.

10.   After the following chapter on a normative framework for decentralization, the rest of this report is organized according to the key issues facing decentralization policy: (a) assignment of public responsibilities by level of government; (b) central/local fiscal relations; (c) financing of local government investments; and (d) local government planning and financial management. The reader should keep in mind that there are considerable overlaps in these issue areas, and policy decisions in one area necessarily affect other issue areas. Table 1, presented on the following two pages, provides a summary of the main recommendations for each of the above issue areas, as presented in Chapters III-VI. The final chapter provides an agenda for implementation of these recommendations.

POLAND: DECENTRALIZATION AND REFORM OF THE STATE
Table 1. Summary of Issues and Recommendations

ISSUE AREA	SPECIFIC ISSUES	RECOMMENDATIONS AND OBSERVATIONS
1. Assignment of Responsibilities	(a) Delegation vs. Decentralization	(i) Keep agenda simple; if significant ambiguities are present regarding assignment, keep centralized in short-term.
		(ii) Local governments should concentrate on infrastructure and services that are clearly local in nature.
		(iii) If Central Government wishes to control service quality and/or price, but with local government delivery, then service should be clearly understood as delegated to local governments -- preferable to have voluntary delegation, with same rules for all local governments, that in turn may "take it or leave it".
	(b) Economic Efficiency vs. Inter-personal equity	(i) During critical transition, keep assignment roles simple, with local governments specializing in economic efficiency (its comparative advantage) and central government in inter-personal equity.
		(ii) When local governments have comparative advantage for implementing central governments's inter-personal equity objective, programs with this objective should be clearly delegated to them.
	(c) Second Tier of Local Government	(i) Second tier probably a good idea, but not in short term; wait until ETP is well advanced and until most of the major issues for implementation of current tier are resolved.
		(ii) During transition, some benefits of second tier of local government could be achieved by defining more clearly Voivodship responsibilities, with at least partial delegation.
	(d) Institutional Intermediary	(i) Need for national institution "in charge" of decentralization policy during transition period.
		(ii) Institutional intermediary chosen may be relatively small, with many functions contracted with private institutions (e.g. foundations, universities, consulting firms).

POLAND: DECENTRALIZATION AND REFORM OF THE STATE
Table 1 (continued)

ISSUE AREA	SPECIFIC ISSUES	RECOMMENDATIONS AND OBSERVATIONS
2. Central/Local Fiscal Relations	(a) Sources of Financing for Local Governments	(i) Priority source of financing should be direct cost recovery from direct beneficiaries -- place local infrastructure and services of "utility" nature on self-financing basis. (ii) Taxes (both national and local) should be financing source of last resort.
	(b) Amount of Fiscal Transfers	(i) Minimize fiscal transfers, given local expenditure responsibilities. (ii) Substitute fiscal transfers with local user charges and fees -- potential savings represent about one-half of current fiscal transfers, or one percent of GDP.
	(c) Subsidies	(i) If Central Government's policy is to provide subsidies to beneficiaries of local infrastructure and services, then (a) don't decentralize or (b) delegate responsibility on voluntary basis with clear rules of game.
	(d) Local Institutional Capacity	(i) With local capacity weak and uneven, keep relationships simple. (ii) In near term, limit local responsibilities to economic efficiency tasks for which local governments have clear comparative advantage. (iii) When there is mix of central/local objectives or comparative advantages, then delegate these tasks only to gminas that accept national standards and financing conditions, including clear and strict limits on fiscal transfers.
3. Financing Local Government Investments	(a) Access to Domestic Financial Sector for Local Investments	(i) Local government financial management information systems should be created as basis for evaluation of local investment proposals and creditworthiness.
	(b) Specialized Institution(s) for municipal lending	(i) Specialized institution has relevant, medium-term role, but it should not have monopoly for municipal lending, and lending should be on commercial terms (ii) Government should discourage or reject municipal banks not subject fully to market discipline. (iii) Government should not establish subsidized lines of credit for local governments or their enterprises.
4. Local Government Planning & Financial Management	(a) Local Institutional Capacity	(i) Local Governments need massive technical assistance program in (a) financial management, (b) expenditure planning and control, (c) procurement and contracting and (d) land management and regulatory functions.

CHAPTER II. NORMATIVE FRAMEWORK

11. Poland's economic transformation program requires simultaneous reforms in several critical areas, including (a) transition from a national tax system based on public enterprises to a modern system based primarily on the value added tax and personal and corporate income taxes, (b) privatization and stimulation of a market economy, (c) decentralization of the state, (d) new intergovernmental fiscal arrangements, and (e) restructuring of the financial sector. Thus, decentralization is taking place in an environment in which it affects other key reform areas, and vice versa.

12. The LSGA provides for the transfer of significant public sector responsibilities to local governments (see Chapter III and Annexes I, II and V). Although the LSGA holds that local government is an autonomous tier of government, with this autonomy protected by the courts, national policies are providing "mixed signals" to local governments regarding the scope of this autonomy. For example, local governments are to have an autonomous budget based on own-source taxes, fees and incomes from local property (LSGA, Chapter 6), yet the Central Government stipulates "caps" on local taxes and public housing rents. Local land management and regulation are considered to be local responsibilities under the LSGA, but other national legislation (existing and proposed) provides that the Central Government retains important controls in this area. This is resulting in confusion that may slow down land market transactions and new private sector investments (Annex VII).

13. Although local government financial management through 1991 may be considered prudent, given the constraints under which local governments are operating (Annex III), there are causes for concern. For example, it is reported that some local governments are attempting to "hide" local revenues (creating extra-budget accounts) because their officials know that if a local government reports higher own-source revenues, this will result in decreased fiscal transfers (Annex I). Furthermore, the Government's proposal to decentralize water supply and sanitation (1992) and primary education (by 1994) represents a significant increase in local government responsibilities. Because of the complexity and importance of decentralization issues within the evolving transformation program, a clear analytic structure is required to evaluate these issues.

14. The LSGA is generally consistent with a decentralized market economy as the cornerstone of the Government's economic transition program, and with the Council of Europe's European Charter of Local Self-Government. However, decentralization is a radical structural change in Polish governance, and past behavior, structures and trends are of limited use in formulating the agenda for the future. Decentralization also involves a complex set of political, historic, economic, financial and administrative factors that in other countries have resulted in conflicts and compromises over decades and even centuries, with significantly different outcomes. Therefore, decentralization and reform of the state must address many issues on which "reasonable people may agree to disagree". This chapter seeks to provide an explicit normative

base on which the analysis of decentralization issues presented in the following chapters is founded.

15.   The LSGA is broadly consistent with the following objectives that serve as a normative framework based primarily on public finance theory applied to Poland's transition program and guided by international experience:

(a)   economic efficiency -- the allocation of local public and quasi-public goods is more efficiently made at the local level where the demand for these goods is more easily identified and rationed;

(b)   equity -- as general principles (i) beneficiaries of local public goods should pay for them (this also is linked strongly to the economic efficiency objective), and (ii) because human resources may migrate across local jurisdictions and because of the national government's concern with human resources for national economic development, minimum levels of expenditures for human resource development should be assured by the national government (at least potentially) in all local jurisdictions (equity is thus defined primarily in inter-personal terms); and

(c)   stability -- decentralization may contribute to macroeconomic stability if (i) local expenditure responsibilities are clearly determined, (ii) local governments have resource mobilization authority consistent with these responsibilities, (iii) central/local fiscal transfers are transparent, predictable and held strictly within sustainable parameters of macroeconomic policy, and (iv) local governments do not borrow on subsidized terms and conditions.

16.   Translating these broad objectives into practical strategies requires judgements on the comparative advantage of each level of government for implementing these objectives. The comparative advantage of local governments regarding each objective is examined below.

17.   Equity. From a general policy perspective, local governments, because of the high degree of openness of their economies, do not have a comparative advantage in formulation of distributional policies -- the target groups are literally moving targets, as people migrate from jurisdiction to jurisdiction. Those goods and services targeted on inter-personal equity (e.g., some human resources and the safety net during transition) should be assigned in principle to the Central Government. As will be noted in Chapter III, however, local governments may have a comparative advantage in delivering some goods and services for implementation of the Central Government's distributional policies, with appropriate guidelines and financing arrangements.

18.   Stability. The fiscal and monetary tools for stabilization policy clearly should rest with the Central Government. Although local governments should not be responsible for stabilization policies, their behavior must be consistent with them. The Central Government must ensure that national legislation for assignment of responsibilities by level of government and for

local resource mobilization provides adequate conditions and incentives for local government performance clearly supportive of stabilization programs.

19.   Efficiency. Local governments have a comparative advantage in providing and financing public and quasi-public goods that are clearly local in impact. This is because citizens may express more effectively their preferences, and willingness to pay, for local goods and services to local governments than to the Central Government. Likewise, the beneficiaries of local goods and services may be more easily identified at the local level.

20.   The key operational concept for local government comparative advantage is accountability. The potential for local governments to be held accountable for equity and stabilization policies is quite limited; for economic efficiency, it is quite high. In this report, accountability goes beyond the narrow interpretation traditionally given to this concept, that elected bodies should be held responsible by their constituents for their decisions and actions (e.g., through elections, transparent budgets and audits). Although this interpretation is extremely important, the accountability concept used here also includes a wider meaning crucial to implementing the efficiency objective: accountability means that local government services are provided to residents in accordance with their preferences and financed mainly by residents to whom the major part of the benefits of the services accrue.

21.   Accountability thus becomes the key operational concept on which to formulate and evaluate decentralization and reform of the state, and it is the primary principle on which the analysis of key decentralization issues is based in the following chapters.

CHAPTER III. ASSIGNMENT OF PUBLIC RESPONSIBILITIES BY LEVEL OF GOVERNMENT

22.   This is the most difficult and significant issue of decentralization. Difficult because there is no generally agreed technical "model" for the assignment question and the issue is fundamentally political, although these political decisions surely may be guided by public finance theory and experience, as noted in Chapter II. Significant because how the assignment issue is resolved sets the basic point of reference for addressing other decentralization issues.

23.   So-called local governments have long existed under the central planning schemes of Poland and other countries. However, there was no effective assignment of responsibilities to local government officials, and hence no accountability of these officials to the people affected by their actions. Therefore, there was no decentralization of the state; rather, the state was deconcentrated (geographic districts of the unitary state) with delegation of some tasks to deconcentrated units of the state, and with accountability flowing from bottom to top in terms of fulfilling central planning tasks.

24.   After less than two years of local government reform implementation, it is not surprising that there are significant ambiguities regarding assignment issues. These ambiguities include conflicting legal and administrative interpretations of central and local responsibilities for many of the areas cited in the LSGA as being the responsibility of local governments: spatial organization, land use and environmental protection; local transport systems; water supply and sanitation; energy and heat; health services; social assistance; housing; kindergarten and primary education; and public order and fire protection.[2] Among the many examples of confusion (further analysis is provided in Annexes II, V and VII) are: local councils set urban bus fares, but Voivodships[3] control parking; water companies are being transferred to local governments, but it is not clear who will determine fees; land development, sub-division, building permits and business licensing involve complex regulations involving both local governments and Voivodships. Following are discussions of key, specific issues within the broad assignment issue area.

A. Delegation versus Decentralization

25.   Poland, with its unitary system of government, should distinguish as clearly as possible between what powers and responsibilities are being decentralized to local government, and those responsibilities that are being delegated. Lack of clarity on this distinction is creating much of the

---

2/ The LSGA is not clear whether some or all of these areas are the exclusive responsibility of local governments, or if they are to be shared with the Central Government.

3/ The 49 Voivodships of Poland are geographical regions of the central administration. They are not an independent tier of government.

ambiguity and confusion about who is really responsible for what. When
certain responsibilities are <u>delegated</u> by the central to local governments,
then local governments are really agents of the central government, and the
predominant flow of accountability is from bottom up. When responsibilities
are <u>decentralized</u>, the higher level of government ceases to have
responsibility, and accountability flows from the local government to its
citizens.

26.   A common difficulty, of course, is when the line between delegation and
decentralization is not clear. For example, under the LSGA, primary education
is to be a "local government responsibility". From a decentralization
perspective, having primary education as an exclusively local government
responsibility may result in economic efficiency (e.g., local expression of
preferences and willingness to pay) and accountability gains. However, if the
Government's policy is to ensure that at least minimum standards of primary
education are achieved nationwide, then full decentralization may not be
appropriate; primary education may remain centralized, or some
responsibilities may be delegated to local governments as administrative
agents of the central governments, with appropriate safeguards (such as
earmarking and performance audits) that delegated tasks are performed
according to national standards.

27.   Ambiguities about delegation versus decentralization are far from unique
to Poland; they are common in all democracies with more than one level of
government. The special condition of Poland is that these ambiguities take
place during an extraordinary transition period in which more pressing
requirements of the macroeconomic program should take precedence, in the short
term, over resolution of these ambiguities. It is therefore <u>recommended</u> that,
when these ambiguities cannot be resolved quickly, the decentralization aim be
compromised in the short term. This means that when in doubt, keep
responsibility at the center, where transaction costs are minimized, and let
the local governments do well those things that are clearly local (e.g., solid
waste, drainage, urban traffic and transport). This is better than to burden
local governments (and potentially waste scarce fiscal resources) with tasks
for which the "rules of the game" concerning central standards, financing and
other interventions are not clear.

28.   When political or administrative concerns are perceived to require some
local government participation in an ambiguous areas, it is <u>recommended</u> that
this be clearly understood as <u>delegation</u>, with the local government acting as
administrative agent of the center. Take the existing public housing stock,
for example. This is considered a matter decentralized to local governments,
yet rents are determined by the Central Government. The Central Government
should not have it both ways. If the Central Government considers that public
housing rent decisions cannot be decentralized to local governments, then
public housing should not be considered a mandatory local service. If the
Central Government decides to wash its hands of the local public housing
stock, then it should give local government full authority and accountability
for rent and other policies. Perhaps a pragmatic solution to the ambiguities
in this and other areas is "voluntary delegation". In this case, the central
government maintains control over standards and prices, but it may delegate
operation to local governments if local governments accept the terms and

conditions of such delegation. This has been the strategy for the transition period, until 1994, regarding primary education. In 1991, 95 of the almost 2,500 local governments accepted the delegated primary education responsibility under the terms and conditions offered by the Ministry of Education.

29.   In summary, without clarity in assignment of responsibilities, there can be no clear accountability. Without clear accountability, many of the potential benefits of decentralization may be transformed into perverse incentives leading to economic destabilization (e.g., unpredictable, negotiated fiscal transfers, subsidized credit lines to local governments, and others as discussed below). Because the urgent issues of the transition program require the full attention of key national policy makers, and because decentralization is too important to leave to "second string" policy makers, the general recommendation for the near term is to focus decentralization on tasks that are clearly local in economic impact, financing and accountability. Over time, as the macroeconomic transition program successfully takes hold, decentralization of more controversial, and generally more important, tasks may be re-evaluated in a more stable macroeconomic environment, where "crisis management" should not divert attention from the important decisions regarding the comparative advantage by level of government for delivery and financing of infrastructure and service systems.

B. Economic Efficiency versus Inter-personal Equity

30.   Alleviating the social costs of transition are of central concern for the Government's transition program (see CEM, Chapter V), and the social sectors are vital to Poland's development[4]. The issue is what role should local governments play in the Government's inter-personal equity objective.

31.   As noted in Chapter II, local governments do not have a comparative advantage in developing distributional policies. As a practical matter, however, local governments may have a comparative advantage in delivering (but not in financing) some services targeted on inter-personal equity, because of their closer contact with and understanding of potential beneficiaries. In these cases, however, delivery responsibility should be clearly understood as delegated to them by the central government, with the appropriate central financing arrangements. In summary, the general recommendation here is the same as that for "delegation versus decentralization": keep responsibility assignments as simple as possible, and based on clear comparative advantages, especially during this critical phase of the transition program when attention should be focused on national stability and economic growth.

C. A Second Tier of Local Government

32.   There is a broad discussion, but no consensus, regarding creation of an additional tier of sub-national government. Currently there are two tiers of government: the Central Government, complemented by 49, deconcentrated,

---

4/ See the World Bank, "Poland: Social Sectors Expenditure Review", Report No. 10158-POL, January 31, 1992.

administrative districts (Voivodships) of this government; and almost 2,500 municipalities (gminas). One proposal is to transform Voivodships into an independent tier of government, with some or all elected officials, expenditure responsibilities and revenue sources. A complement to this proposal is to realign Voivodship boundaries to roughly coincide with the Powiat jurisdictions that existed before World War II and, with modifications, until the early 1970s.

33. Creating a second tier of local government in Poland probably is a good idea; most OECD countries have more than one tier of local government. The real issue is timing. Poland has less than two years of experience with one tier of local government, and there are many, understandable ambiguities regarding responsibility assignment. Creation of a second tier before the current first tier of local government is reasonably "absorbed" runs the risk of creating more confusion than benefits. With the same basic reasoning applied to previous issues, it is recommended that a second tier not be created until after overcoming the currently acute problems in the implementation of the Government's transition program, achieving the fiscal and price stability aims noted in the CEM, and until most of the major issues regarding implementation of the current tier are resolved. In the meantime, some benefits of a second local tier could be achieved through more clearly defining responsibilities of Voivodships, and when appropriate provide at least partial delegation of central government responsibilities to them. This would appear to be appropriate for the roads sector, for example, where operation and maintenance could be delegated to Voivodships under clear national guidelines, thus achieving some benefits of expenditure efficiency resulting from deconcentrated management, without the disruptive political and administrative costs of creating a second tier of government. Also, the LSGA provides that local governments may come together to form associations for delivery and financing of infrastructure or services of a regional coverage. France, with about 36,000 municipalities, has a broad experience with such associations. See Annex II, Section D, for additional analysis.

D. Institutional Intermediary

34. What Polish institutions are capable of addressing the full range of issues regarding assignment responsibilities noted above? And which of these institutions are capable of designing and implementing policies for decentralization of the Polish state? The Ministry of Finance has taken a lead role through its budgeting function. Although the state budget is an important and necessary interface between levels of government (see central/local fiscal relations below), it is far from sufficient to address broad decentralization issues. Furthermore, it should not, because broad decentralization policy is not the responsibility of the Ministry of Finance.

35. The answer to the two questions of the preceding paragraph is that no institution is "in charge" of decentralization policy. Responsibilities are fractioned and accountability diluted. The Office for Local Governments of the Council of Ministers has undertaken a coordination role, and until this year had representatives for local government affairs in each Voivodship. This Office has been very weak, however, as it has basically reacted to Ministry of Finance determinations and has not been aggressively addressing

the broad range of decentralization issues required to make these consistent with the transition program and to achieve the potential benefits of decentralization.

36. Should there be a national institution "in charge" of decentralization policy? Is there not a fundamental contradiction between decentralization and a strong central institution to promote it? International experience (e.g., Chile, Argentina, Ecuador) indicates that a strong national institution as "principal agent" for decentralization is important, especially at the beginning of a significant shift in assignment of responsibilities by level of government. Thus, an institution "in charge" is an important element missing now in Poland. Current proposals to focus broad public sector reform in general, and decentralization policy in particular, in the Ministry of Interior could close this institutional gap. To do so, the primary responsibilities of a "Municipal Development Agency" should be:

(a) to propose to the Council of Ministers

  (i) a strategy (with implementing legislation) for phasing in increased local government responsibilities in a manner fully consistent with the Government's economic transition program, and overall fiscal constraint,

  (ii) removal of all national interventions in local government autonomy (e.g., national caps on local taxes and fees) that are not consistent with (i),

  (iii) measures to ensure that local governments have the authority to establish local revenue bases and rates fully consistent with their responsibilities, and

  (iv) intergovernmental fiscal transfers fully consistent with (i);

(b) to provide to all local governments an authoritative source of information on what are current and proposed national policies, laws, regulations, etc.;

(c) to receive from all local governments their reactions and inputs on how (a) and (b) should be improved;

(d) to develop a national information system for local governments, including comparative data (across gminas and over time) on finances, expenditure performance, personnel effectiveness, etc., and

(e) to manage the technical assistance and training program (financed with national and international sources) required to strengthen national and local institutions in order to implement effectively the strategy for increased local government responsibilities.

37. In order to discharge effectively these responsibilities, the proposed Municipal Development Agency (MDA) would need to have considerable authority and access to information and decision making processes, particularly those

relating to the economic transition program and other measures regarding reform of the state. The MDA would not need to be a large entity. For example, many of the functions for which it would be responsible could be contracted with one or more universities, foundations or consulting firms. Contracting out for as much as possible would be sensible because the responsibilities of this institutional intermediary should decrease substantially over time.

38.   In summary, it is <u>recommended</u> that the Government make a commitment to identify an existing entity or to create such an entity for proposing and managing its strategy for decentralization, including the integration of this strategy with the Government's economic transition program and with other specific measures to reform the Polish state. Current proposals to focus decentralization policy and reform of central/local relations in the Ministry of Interior could be timely and effective if they include a MDA with the characteristics noted above. The MDA also could have an important, transitory role in financing local government investments, as noted in Chapter V below.

CHAPTER IV. CENTRAL/LOCAL FISCAL RELATIONS

A. Linkages with the Transition Program

39.   The CEM cites the risk of a return to hyperinflation as the predominant danger for undermining the transition program, with potentially disastrous results. Without significant corrections in current fiscal trends, the non-financial public sector deficit may reach 11 percent of GDP in 1992, presenting a clear and present danger of igniting runaway inflation (CEM, p. 9).

40.   But how does local government reform fit into this macroeconomic and fiscal policy picture? Based on preliminary results for 1991 and crude projections for 1992, local governments account for about 11 percent of total public sector expenditures, or about 4 percent of GDP.[5] Local government expenditures are financed roughly as follows:

    50 percent from local government own-source revenues (about 30-40 percent local taxes and 10-20 percent fees, and sale and rental of gmina properties);

    25 percent from shared national taxes (various enterprise taxes in 1991 and shares of the personal and corporate income taxes in 1992); and

    25 percent from fiscal transfers (about 15 percent transferred as block grants including equalization criteria, and 10 percent earmarked).

Therefore, the Central Government is providing financing for about one-half of total local expenditures, or two percent of GDP. What are the prospects for reducing this fiscal burden, bringing local government reform policy more in line with the transition program at a crossroads juncture, without undermining the Government's policy for decentralization and reform of the state? To answer this, it is useful to examine the expenditure pattern of local governments.

41.   The financial accounting and reporting systems of local governments are woefully lacking and make analyses over time and between local governments extremely difficult at best. However, visits to gminas in December 1991 provide "orders of magnitude" regarding how local governments are allocating their resources:[6]

5/ An overview of local government finance in Poland's public sector is provided in Annex I. This includes a review of local government finance legislation.

6/ This allocation distribution is based on data collected in the gminas Kielce (214,000 population, and with executed budget for January-November 1991) and Radom (250,000 population, and with planned expenditures for 1991,

Expenditure Category		% of Total Expenditures
-- Current Expenditures		
Administration		10
Education (Kindergartens and nurseries)		20
Road maintenance, street lighting, etc.		9
Parks, culture, sports, welfare		6
Other direct expenditures		8
Subsidies to "decentralized" entities[7], of which		27
public transport	13	
housing	10	
solid waste	4	
-- Capital Expenditures		20
TOTAL EXPENDITURES		100

42. Perhaps the most important way to link the urgent requirements of the transition program with the long-term objectives of decentralization and reform of the state is to apply the following principle: fiscal sources should be considered the revenue of last resort, especially for local goods and services considered to be in the public domain and for which demand may be rationed through prices.

43. This principle, of direct cost recovery from direct beneficiaries, may be applied to (a) subsidies for public transport, housing and solid waste and (b) at least a portion of capital expenditures. Together, these account for about one-half of total gmina expenditures. If direct cost recovery could be achieved for at least one-half of these expenditures, plus other expenditures for which user charges could be applied (e.g., kindergartens and nurseries for families without justification of subsidy, admission fees for some park, cultural and sports activities), a substitution of fiscal resources with local user fees and charges for about 25 percent of total local expenditures appears to be achievable in the near term. In other words, enhanced local government cost recovery could represent a fiscal savings for the central government on the order of one percent of GDP, without sacrifice to local services, and with the added benefit of enhancing local government accountability for those services financed predominantly with local resources.

---

excluding earmarked funds for primary education). These are roughly representative of urban gminas that account for approximately one-third of the total number of gminas and about 60 percent to Poland's total population.

7/ These decentralized entities, or satellites, are considered as gmina "enterprises" and subsidies may appear as a relatively clear transfer from the gmina budget to them. When services of an "enterprise" nature are not decentralized from the gmina budget, they appear as a "direct" gmina expenditure. In the latter case, actual service-specific subsidies are hard to estimate; this is particularly the case in smaller gminas. Annex II provides details.

44. Local cost recovery could provide savings for the central budget on the same order of magnitude as cited in the CEM (para. 45) for postponement of wage increases, curtailment of housing subsidies[8], and temporary drop in investment. To achieve this magnitude of fiscal savings through decentralization, however, the "rules of the game" with respect to local expenditure, financing and regulatory authorities, as discussed in the preceding section, will have to be made much more clear and implemented effectively.

B. Recommendations

45. When feasible, the first source of financing for local infrastructure and services should be fees from beneficiaries. When financing by fees is feasible, the private sector may participate through ownership, concession, management contract, or other arrangements. The second source of financing should be local taxes and other revenues. The Central Government should ensure that local governments have a tax base and rate setting authority consistent with their expenditure responsibilities, and then the Central Government should provide incentives for local resource mobilization. The first and best incentive that the Central Government may provide is to have central/local fiscal transfers clearly limited and allocated on a very simple and transparent basis.

46. Having central/local fiscal transfers limited, predictable and allocated among local governments in a simple and "fair" manner cannot be overemphasized during the critical transition period. As noted above, central transfers could be reduced by at least one percent of GDP if the following decentralization policy is implemented: local infrastructure and services of a "utility" nature will no longer receive financing from national taxes; local governments are free to set up (through privatization, concessions, etc., the Central Government is not concerned with these details, as these are exclusively local in responsibility[9]) entities that will be administratively independent and financially autonomous.

47. If certain "lifeline" rates (e.g., for water, public transportation, heating) for households that fall below a clearly defined poverty line are decided to be subsidized, then there appear to be three basic alternatives. The first, and generally preferred, alternative is to have a tariff structure that provides cross-subsidies. For example, a water company may have low tariffs for consumption up to an established level considered appropriate for a "lifeline" policy, so that poor households could consume up to this quantity with a subsidized tariff. This limited subsidy could be "recovered" through

---

8/ These are primarily directed through the financial sector (see CEM, Chapter 4), so that reduced housing rent subsidies through gmina budgets would reduce total subsidies to the housing sector even further.

9/ In order to implement such measures, however, the Central Government would need to provide the legal and regulatory "enabling environment" required for local public utilities to be administratively independent and financially autonomous.

higher tariffs on larger amounts of water consumed. This provides for self-financing of a "closed" utility. The other alternatives provide for an "open" utility in financing terms, with external (other than utility beneficiaries) financing for part of the utility cost. This of course introduces considerable complexity in pricing and subsidies, and as a general principle this should be avoided, especially during the transition period. However, if the Government has a strong policy to provide lifeline subsidy rates that are large and would be provided to a large proportion of beneficiaries, then it probably is desirable to keep the service at the Central Government (or Voivodship) level, because local government is not the best level for redistribution policy (para. 17). Finally, if the utility responsibility is decentralized to local government, and if there is a national policy to subsidize some beneficiaries, then there need to be clear rules of the game. These might be:

(a)   the local government is responsible for placing the local utility on a self-financing basis; and

(b)   the central government is responsible for providing subsidies to the target population. In this case, the subsidy may be provided through

   (i)   some form of voucher to the beneficiary, or

   (ii)   an earmarked fiscal transfer to the local government for the subsidy. In this case, it would be important for the central government to establish the terms and conditions that would apply to all local governments for these earmarked subsidies. In this way, there would be no case-by-case negotiation for subsidies (blurring transparency and accountability, with potential partisan political influence), and local governments would be in a position to "take it or leave it", much as is the case now with primary education. If a local government takes the subsidy, it is fully responsible and accountable to its constituents for the quality and coverage of the service and to the Central Government as its implementing agent for a delegated service (subsidy administration). If the local government refuses to take the task of administrative agent of the central government under the terms and conditions offered to it (and all other local governments), then the central government may use a voucher system, or it may keep that service centralized (central ministry or Voivodship) until alternative terms and conditions for delegation or decentralization may be agreed.

48.   For financing of local infrastructure or services of a public or quasi-public nature (e.g., roads, streets, traffic management, drainage, public lighting and cleaning, parks) local taxes should be the preferred source of financing. Polish local governments have a significant potential for expanding the local tax base, making it more equitable and managing it more effectively. To achieve this potential, however, the Central Government should remove constraints to local tax policy (e.g., caps on urban property tax based on area) and allow an expanded local tax base (e.g., inclusion of

rural properties). Details of these recommendations are provided in Chapter VI and Annexes VI and VIII.

49.   Implementation of these recommendations, to (a) place local utilities on a self-financing basis and (b) make local taxation policy and administration consistent with local responsibilities for public infrastructure and services, would allow the Central Government to focus on its comparative advantage in local government finance. This is in providing a "level playing field" for all local governments, or tax "equalization" policy. The Central Government's role, through the proposed Municipal Development Agency, would be to develop and implement, through the Ministry of Finance after approval by the Council of Ministers, a revenue sharing system that would provide national revenues to those local governments that have a local tax base insufficient to finance local public goods that have been assigned to them.

50.   To implement fully such a revenue sharing system, however, a local government financial management information system (see para. 36) will be required. Given the other recommendations of this report, the proposed revenue sharing system would be (a) strictly limited by national fiscal constraints and only for equalization purposes limited to local public goods, and (b) transparent and predictable through a formula-driven distribution among local governments based on local tax base, and provided only to those local governments that can not meet their service delivery obligations given the limitations of their local tax base. With this limited role for central government financing of local responsibilities, fiscal transfers could be limited to 10-20 percent of local revenues and held under one percent of GDP.

V. FINANCING LOCAL GOVERNMENT INVESTMENTS

A. Issues

51.   In order to make significant investments in a timely and efficient manner, creditworthy gminas and their enterprises should leverage their savings with prudent borrowing. This is recognized in the LSGA. Currently, however, Poland's financial sector is not providing long-term credit to local governments because the financial sector is just now beginning to restructure on a market economy basis (CEM, Chapter IV), and also because the assignment of expenditure responsibilities and financing arrangements for local governments is not clear.

52.   Over time, Poland's capital markets should be responsive to the investment financing needs of creditworthy local governments (and their enterprises), and these should compete with alternative financing demands (e.g., agriculture, industry, commerce). This begs the question, however, of what is to be done in the transition period when the domestic financial sector should be strengthened along with local financial management capacity on which commercial creditworthiness may be based. The reform transition strategy needs to address this issue in order to avoid potentially strong pressures from local governments for increased fiscal transfers on an ad hoc and discretionary basis and/or direct central government financing of local investments that would undermine local autonomy and the financial discipline required by the Government's economic transition program. However, unless local governments have predictable local own-source and shared revenues and a well defined financial accounting and reporting system, financial institutions will be unable to evaluate their creditworthiness. These requirements for a sustainable, fiscally responsible system of financing local government investments highlight the priority of clearly defining local government expenditure responsibilities, central/local fiscal relations, and the need to strengthen local institutional capacity in order to have an efficient linking of private and public sector behavior.

B. Recommendations

53.   In this transition period, with simultaneous reform in central/local relations and in the financial sector, the phasing in of reform elements is critical. In the long term, the financing of local investments primarily from domestic capital markets will be very important for two basic reasons: first, this provides an effective leveraging of local savings without fiscal distortions, and second, this would impose market discipline on local government financial management. In the short term, it is important to lay the foundations on which these medium and long term benefits may be achieved, and to avoid initiating policies and/or institutions that may undermine these longer term benefits.

54.   In the near term, two basic initiatives should be undertaken. First, local government expenditure planning and financial accounting, reporting and auditing systems must be put in place and in practice so that local government planning and execution are transparent and the creditworthiness of local

government investment proposals may be evaluated -- these financial management issues are addressed in the following Chapter and in Annexes VI-VIII.

55.   The second initiative is to develop within the Polish financial sector the capacity to evaluate the commercial risk of local investments. Evaluation of municipal creditworthiness is quite different from that of an industrial, agricultural or commercial enterprise. Fortunately, there are many municipal credit institutions throughout the world that may facilitate the transfer of know-how to Polish institutions. For example, the recently created (June 1990) Credit Local d'Europe brings together the principal institutions specialized in financing local governments of Belgium, France, Germany, Italy and Spain as an "European Economic Interest Grouping", and this might be an appropriate vehicle to mobilize technical assistance to the Polish financial sector and to local governments in the area of financing capital improvements programs.

56.   There is some considerable debate about the long-term efficacy of specialized, directed credit institutions. Of course, with perfect information and mobility of factors of production, there would be no debate, as the financial sector could be a completely neutral captor and allocator of savings. The critical issues in Poland, however, are short and medium term, and the key is to promote private sector financing of municipal investments on terms and conditions that promote economic efficiency. This is a much preferred alternative to having Central Government grants and/or subsidized lines of credit to municipalities (often decided through partisan politics) to finance local capital improvements programs.

57.   It is not clear when the restructuring financial sector may be able to provide adequate investment financing for local governments. In the short term (say, over the next five years), it may be useful to consider expanding the role of the proposed Municipal Development Agency (MDA) beyond the policy and technical assistance roles outlined in Section D of Chapter III. This Agency could provide long-term loans to eligible municipalities, using one or more banks as financial agent (and not as financial intermediary, until the financial sector is strengthened).

58.   There would be two basic alternatives for financing sources of these loans. First, the Government could designate some part of the "savings" in fiscal transfers to be achieved through improved local cost recovery and tax administration, as recommended in the previous chapter, and provide these to the MDA for its municipal loan program. An alternative, or complementary, financing source, could be borrowing from international development institutions. With either financing alternative, the MDA's loan program would be clearly transitory in nature (until the financial sector is strengthened and responsive to local investment financing demand) and directed to the following objectives:

(a)   substitute current grants financed with national fiscal revenues (and potentially with the inflation tax) with loans;

(b)   provide incentives, through long-term loans currently not available from the financial sector, for local governments to generate savings that may be leveraged for expanded capital improvements programs; and

(c)   initiate the institutional capacity within Poland to evaluate municipal creditworthiness, with this capacity to be transferred to municipalities and to the private financial sector as it stabilizes and is strengthened.

59.   The MDA would incorporate some of the characteristics of the Municipal Development Fund proposed by the Government as part of the local government finance law for 1992. Although Parliament did not approve creation of this Fund, the proposed MDA would focus on decentralization policy, municipal institutional strengthening and limited lending on a transition basis.[10]

60.   Poland's MDA could perform essentially the same functions that have proved helpful to strengthening local government reform in several Latin American countries during severe macroeconomic adjustment periods. For example, the World Bank currently is supporting local government projects through institutions similar to the proposed MDA in Argentina, Brazil and Ecuador, and these projects are demonstrating encouraging implementation results.

61.   Because of the uncertain macroeconomic environment and of the novelty of the proposed MDA's functions, a pilot lending operation may be prudent. For example, a pilot operation could be limited to some three to six gminas (or associations of gminas). The pilot gminas could be chosen so as to include those from cities, towns and villages, in order to acquire experience in gminas with a broad range of investment financing and institutional needs. The pilot project could be launched with a technical assistance program available to all gminas that request it. Interested gminas would then present to the MDA their "Financial Action and Investment Plans" (FAIP), that would be used to select pilot gminas. The financial action part of the FAIP could include measures to: (a) increase local cost recovery and place local enterprises on a financially autonomous and independently managed basis; (b) enhance local tax mobilization and make it more equitable; (c) implement local budgeting, accounting, reporting and auditing procedures according to guidelines to be provided by the MDA; (d) increase expenditure efficiency, including technical, economic, financial and environmental evaluation of maintenance and investment programs; and (e) implement competitive contract preparation, management and supervision. Approved investments proposed under the FAIP would be eligible for MDA loans. Technical assistance to the MDA, and perhaps other key central agencies, also could be part of the pilot project.

10/ The proposed MDA would not, however, be financed with mandatory transfers to it by "rich" gminas, and it would not provide earmarked grants or acquire equity in local enterprises, as contemplated for the Municipal Development Fund.

62.   Selection of the pilot gminas could be made by an panel of national and/or international experts, according to guidelines to be provided by the MDA. Even gminas not selected for the pilot project would benefit through technical assistance available to all gminas, as preparation of a FAIP will be required of all gminas that seek to strengthen their institutional autonomy and efficiency in a decentralized public sector. If such a pilot operation is successful, a follow-up project could be considered, perhaps with all gminas potentially eligible to receive investment financing, and also with emphasis on transferring "lessons learned" to private financial institutions that should substitute MDA investment financing with their own.

63.   In summary, reforms in the mechanisms for financing local government investments encompass three broad areas according to priority. In the long term, the Government should promote access by local governments to domestic capital markets as part of the restructuring of the financial sector. In the medium term, it should support the capacity of banking institutions to provide long-term credit to municipalities, and in the short term, the MDA should provide (a) incentives and technical assistance for promoting municipal creditworthiness and (b) initial lending for filling the financing gap of local investments. The Government also should avoid initiating policies or creating institutions that could undermine responsible local borrowing. Specifically, it should discourage or reject:

(a)   creation of municipal banks that are not subject fully to market discipline -- in other countries there have been too many cases of banks controlled by local or regional governments that have been unable to resist financing local government current account deficits, unjustified investments or even activities such as incumbent's election campaigns; such activities can destabilize national economies (e.g., Argentina, Brazil) when local government banks have special rediscount or overdraft privileges at the Central Bank -- with its transition program at a crossroads, Poland does not need what may appear as "innocent" local government initiatives that can evolve into perverse instruments of central/local partisan politics with very high macroeconomic and social costs; and

(b)   subsidized lines of credit for local governments or their enterprises -- if the Government wishes to subsidize certain activities under local jurisdiction as part of its social policy, these subsidies should be provided through transparent budget allocations and not through the financial sector.

VI. LOCAL GOVERNMENT PLANNING AND FINANCIAL MANAGEMENT

64.   If the Polish society is to receive the benefits of improved efficiency, equity and stability offered by an effective decentralization and reform of the state, the key actors are local governments themselves. The preceding areas of responsibility assignment, central/local fiscal relations and local investment financing may be considered prerequisites for effective decentralization. These prerequisites are largely under the control of the Central Government, and they establish the basic, mostly financial, incentives for local government behavior consistent with the Government's transition program. Thus, the local governments themselves must be the key executing agents of a successful decentralization process.

65.   During the transition period, however, the Central Government has a key role in not only providing incentives for, but also directly supporting, local government institutional strengthening, especially in the following areas (details are provided in Annex VI).

66.   Financial Management. To enhance expenditure efficiency and public accountability for their actions, local governments need to design and implement

(a)   budgeting systems that serve as a link between ends and means, and that provide the base for financial reporting, accounting and auditing procedures;

(b)   strategies for the role, ownership and management of local public utilities;

(c)   local revenue policies and administration, including a significantly strengthened tax management system; and

(d)   systems for monitoring and control of expenditures.

67.   Expenditure Planning and Control. One of the economic arguments in support of decentralization of the public sector is that local governments may ration demand and produce many services more efficiently. However, for this potential to be realized, local governments must have the technical capacity to design service systems, generate and evaluate alternatives, and implement in a cost-effective manner investment and maintenance programs. This capacity is lacking in most gminas.

68.   Procurement and Contracting. Because competitive procurement is an activity intimately linked to a market economy, it is not surprising that there is an almost total lack of capability to undertake a modern procurement process, even in larger local governments. A lack of legal structure and guidelines also is constraining the local capacity to enter into effective contractual agreements for the purchase of works, goods and services.

69.   Land Management and Regulatory Functions. To discharge their responsibilities for spatial organization, land use and environmental

protection, local governments must develop and strengthen their capacity to manage land, particularly in the areas of privatization and promotion of sustainable economic development. Local government regulation should seek to promote public health and safety without placing unnecessary constraints on private sector development.

CHAPTER VII. CONCLUSIONS AND AN AGENDA FOR IMPLEMENTATION

70.   The principal conclusion of this report is that decentralization should
proceed on a gradual and selective basis. Only those tasks for which local
governments have a clear comparative advantage over the central government
should be decentralized during the critical transition period now at a
crossroads. The fundamental comparative advantage of local governments is in
infrastructure and services that are clearly local in impact and for which
beneficiaries of these services are the exclusive, or at least predominant,
source of their financing. This means that local governments should focus on
services for which local officials may be held fully accountable to their
citizens, with this accountability including quality, coverage and financing
of services. If accountability for services delivered by local governments is
blurred and perceived to be a mix of central and local responsibilities, this
may open a "pandora's box" leading to ad hoc, negotiated grants to local
governments and/or pressures for the central government to grant subsidized
lines of credit to local governments, either of which could lead to
destabilizing results inconsistent with the Government's transition program in
general, and with the specific need for fiscal retrenchment emphasized in the
CEM.

71.   In order to develop further decentralization policy and to "manage" the
decentralization process, designation or creation of a Municipal Development
Agency (MDA) is recommended. The head of the MDA should be of Minister or
Vice-Minister rank because decentralization issues cut across areas under the
responsibility of sectoral ministries, and the MDA's head should have
sufficient authority to address effectively issues that may affect the role
and functions of these ministries, as well as of the Ministry of Finance.
Because effective decentralization must be linked to the real and financial
sectors, it may be useful to have a MDA "Consultation Board" or "Steering
Committee" appointed by the Prime Minister, composed of Vice Ministers of key
sectoral ministries, of the Ministry of Finance and of representatives of
local governments and the private sector, and with the objective of improved
coordination of decentralization policy formulation and implementation across
sectors of the Central Government, between levels of government, and with the
private sector.

72.   As noted in para. 37, the MDA would not need to be a large agency, but
it should be able to address a broad range of decentralization issues. In
this regard, it would be important for the MDA to be the Central Government's
single agency for formulation of decentralization policy and for oversight of
implementation measures. A proliferation of "special interest" agencies or
funds dealing primarily with infrastructure or services under local government
responsibility would undermine a coherent decentralization policy effectively
linked to the Government's transition program. Therefore, it is recommended
that the Government consolidate special assistance to local governments under
the "umbrella" of the MDA. This would apply, for example, to the critical,
new areas of local government responsibilities for primary education and water
supply and sanitation.

73.   As noted in Section D of Chapter III, many of the MDA's functions would be transitory and phased out over time, as the economy stabilizes and key decentralization issues are addressed effectively. In order to implement the recommendations made in this report, "terms of reference" for the MDA are proposed below, focussing on the short-term needs to initiate the implementation process. It should be stressed that these terms of reference are indicative, but it is hoped that they may support the Government/Bank dialogue in the decentralization area. In this spirit, the reader should note that

(a)   the "terms of reference" for the proposed MDA assume that it would be the Government's "apex" institution for formulating and proposing decentralization policy to the Council of Ministers, and for overseeing the implementation of this policy; the MDA would not be the key executing agency for the Government's decentralization policy; this would lie with the Ministry of Finance, and some sectoral ministries (e.g., covering education, water supply) and Voivodships for delegated tasks; the MDA could be the executing agency for technical assistance and for pilot lending operations to local governments; and the local governments themselves would be the key executing agents of decentralization policy;

(b)   the terms of reference reflect the current status of decentralization and emphasize the short-term; there will be a transition period of uncertain length, during which the pace of reform may vary across local governments with different characteristics, and these differences will be reflected also in the role and functions of the MDA; and

(c)   therefore the MDA's terms of reference should be interpreted as an initial "roadmap" that should be consistently up-dated and improved as the terrain of decentralization is better understood.

A. Immediate Actions

74.   Within the broad responsibilities noted for the MDA proposed in para. 36, it is recommended that the following concerns be placed at the top of the list of priorities.

(a)   <u>Re-evaluate the scope and pace of decentralization</u>. Through 1991, the responsibilities assigned to and effectively assumed by local governments may be considered as having a predominantly local impact (e.g., solid waste, urban public transport, local roads, streets, drainage, etc.). Over 1992 and 1993, primary education is expected to be transferred to local governments. This raises critical issues of sharply increasing recurrent costs of local governments, and how these are to be financed. If primary education is to be financed substantially through fiscal transfers, this will require a much more demanding revenue sharing system than that contemplated in para. 50 (fiscal transfers in the range of 10-20 percent of local revenues and held under one percent of GDP). This also may increase substantially the number of municipal employees during a period in which broad civil service reform will be considered and perhaps implemented. The MDA should weigh the costs and benefits of such a dramatic increase in local government responsibility. If continued decentralization of primary education is confirmed, perhaps an extended period of the current practice of "voluntary delegation" of primary education to local governments would be prudent.[11] Similar reasoning may be applied to transferring water supply and sanitation responsibilities. If local governments (individually or through associations of gminas) may place newly transferred water and sanitation companies on a self-financing basis in a reasonably short period of time, then local government assumption of this responsibility would be consistent with the recommendations of this report. If, however, as noted in para. 47, the Government's policy will be to provide significant subsidies to substantial consumers, then transfer of water company assets to local governments may provide more economic and social costs than benefits, as rather sophisticated financing mechanisms would need to be implemented across levels of government. As with primary education, the MDA should weigh alternatives, and perhaps voluntary delegation would be a prudent short- to medium-term course.

(b) Remove unnecessary constraints to local government autonomy. A simple but significant undertaking of the MDA would be to classify each responsibility assigned to local governments as decentralized or delegated (see Section A, Chapter III). For decentralized tasks, local governments should have full autonomy over standards, fees, rents, tariffs, etc., as well as a local tax base and rate-setting authority to finance services when direct cost recovery through user charges is not feasible. Local governments should be fully accountable to their beneficiaries for the design, delivery and financing of decentralized infrastructure and services, with the limited exceptions of local governments that do not have a tax base sufficiently broad and buoyant to finance fully local public goods. The MDA should evaluate the legislative capacity of local governments to finance decentralized responsibilities, and propose removal of unnecessary constraints on, and/or enabling legislation to make local resource mobilization consistent with decentralized responsibilities. It also should propose revenue sharing arrangements for tax equalization across local governments, along the lines recommended in paras. 49-50. After key policy decisions have been made regarding assignment of responsibilities, the Bank could provide assistance to the MDA to ensure that international "best practices" and experiences are incorporated in

---

11/ "Voluntary delegation" does not resolve the issues of (a) increasing local responsibility for activities, such as primary education, with extra-municipal (equity) impacts, and (b) the resulting prospect that fiscal transfers become greater than the level noted above (10-20 percent of local revenues). However, it at least may restrict additional fiscal transfers (beyond the "equalization" function noted in paras. 49-50) during the transition to only those gminas that are willing and able to contract for a delegated function, and to assume full accountability. If the conditions of supply are the same for all gminas, and these accept voluntarily the supply conditions, then this presents approximations of a "quasi market", albeit limited.

such a revenue sharing system. For tasks classified by the MDA as
essentially delegated to local governments, at least in the short- to
medium-term, the MDA should propose "rules of the game" for this
delegation, including lines of accountability, standards and financing
arrangements, as discussed in Section A of Chapter III. Voluntary
delegation is an option to be explored. After the political decisions
regarding delegation versus decentralization have been made, the MDA
could benefit from international experience on practical means through
which delegated responsibilities may best be discharged.

(c)   Develop a local government financial management information system. In
      order to monitor local government finances, improve decentralization
      policies and to gain local government access to financial markets, the
      MDA should propose standard municipal financial planning, accounting,
      reporting and audit systems compatible with western standards. The
      IMF's Manual on Government Finance Statistics would be a good guideline
      for these proposals, and international technical assistance could be
      mobilized to assist the MDA in designing and implementing this system.

(d)   Design and implement a comprehensive program of technical assistance.
      As noted above, the MDA itself could be the object of significant
      technical assistance. As noted in Chapter VI, the agenda for technical
      assistance to local governments is large and significant, and detailed
      recommendations are provided in Annex VI. Many bi-lateral and
      international development institutions are eager to provide technical
      assistance for Poland's decentralization, and some already are doing so.
      The MDA's role would be to define priorities and target technical
      assistance in the most effective manner possible. The MDA should
      distinguish between technical assistance that may be most effectively
      provided with local resources, and that for which international
      assistance would be most appropriate. In order for international
      assistance to be most effective, the MDA should inform potential donors
      of priority areas for which technical assistance is requested. Of
      course, individual local governments may arrange for their own technical
      assistance programs without MDA intervention or support, but the MDA
      could assume the useful role of "clearing house" for large scale
      international assistance.

B. Medium-Term Strategy

75.   The key item on the medium-term agenda is to promote financing of local
government (including local utility enterprises) investments by the private
financial sector. Although implementation may be considered medium-term, the
MDA should lay immediately the foundation on which this strategy may be
implemented. For example, the MDA should monitor proposals regarding the
creation of municipal banks or subsidized lines of credit for local
governments or their enterprises, and discourage or recommend rejection of
these proposals, as noted in para. 63. Also, the information system
recommended in (c) above should be designed with a view to promote evaluation
of municipal creditworthiness. Finally, the MDA should consider designing a
pilot lending operation for local governments, along the lines suggested in
Chapter V.

ANNEXES

ANNEX I

OVERVIEW OF LOCAL GOVERNMENT FINANCE IN POLAND'S PUBLIC SECTOR

1.   The present system of public finance is in a stage of transition. The
new system put in place for 1991 will be changed once the Personal Income Tax
(PIT) and the Value Added Tax (VAT) are introduced. The introduction of the
new taxation system will radically transform existing tax bases. The
government shelved the plan to introduce VAT in 1992 arguing that a
simultaneous implementation of VAT and PIT would exert pressures on its
limited administrative capacities. The PIT law was passed by the parliament,
and is scheduled to be introduced in 1992. The introduction of PIT will
eliminate several shared national revenue instruments. Yet, some principles
underlying the current local financial framework are to be retained. For this
reason, it is useful to identify and assess intergovernmental fiscal
relations, local government's (gmina) revenue base, the extent of fiscal
autonomy and local financial management, and local government financial system
proposed for 1992.

2.   The local financing system, introduced in 1991, was a first step to
assure financial autonomy of gminas stipulated in the Local Self-Government
Act of 1990. The legal foundations for implementation of this Act were
provided by three laws: the Act on Revenues of Gminas and Rules of Financing
(passed by the Sejm on December 14, 1990); the Budget Act (January 5, 1991);
and the Act on Taxes and Local Fees (January 12, 1991). These Acts separated
local budgets from the state budget and simplified the public finance system
by abolishing extra-budgetary arrangements and by linking sources of financing
with assigned tasks. Viovodship budgets are now fully incorporated in the
state budget (after elimination of Voivodship shares of enterprise taxes), and
except for the local block grant, gmina finances are no longer a component of
the state budget. The budget law for 1991 has increased the fiscal autonomy
of gminas and introduced greater transparency in intergovernmental transfers
than under the previous system. The local budget law for 1992 maintains the
same structure as the 1991 law, with modifications as noted below.

3.   Although the 1991 local government financial system has introduced a
considerable degree of fiscal decentralization, it should be noted that local
fiscal autonomy is restricted by upper limits set by the Central Government on
local tax rates and fees, as well as by central determination of agricultural
tax rates. The latter tax accounts for a significant portion of own-source
revenues of rural gminas. For example, it accounted for 24 percent of planned
revenues of Jablonna (population 8,000) visited by the mission.

A. Revenue Flows to Gmina Budgets

4.   The current system of local financing consists of the following revenue
sources: own-source revenues; shared national taxes; and fiscal transfers from
the central budget. The basic structure for 1992 is the same as for 1991,
except that shared enterprise taxes (1991) are replaced by shared personal and
income taxes in 1992. These sources have been estimated for the 1991 state

budget (see Table 1). Included in these estimates are (a) gmina revenues from sale or leasing of gmina assets, and (b) amounts negotiated and transferred to gminas from Voivodships or the Ministry of Education (via the state budget, currently estimated at 0.1 trillion Zl) to finance assigned or delegated functions from the State Administration. Estimates of the intergovernmental fiscal flow of funds in 1991 are presented in Figure 1, with details provided in Table 1.

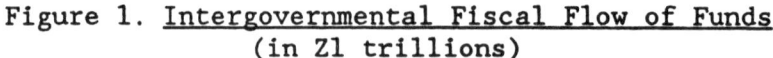

Figure 1. Intergovernmental Fiscal Flow of Funds
(in Zl trillions)

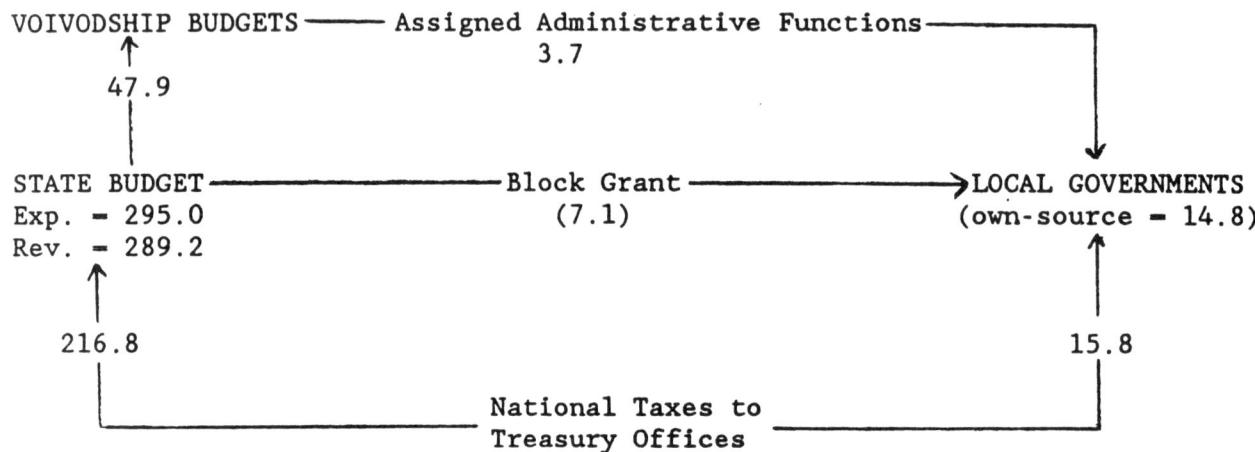

5.   All national domestic taxes and some local taxes and fees are collected by treasury offices and then transferred to state and local budgets. Local taxes and fees paid to the Treasury Offices (Zl 3.0 trillion planned for 1991, and included in local own-source revenues of Figure 1) include: inheritance and gift tax; administrative charges; lump-sum taxes; and dividend/levy on capital assets of gmina-owned enterprises. Other local taxes and fees are paid directly to gminas. No changes are envisaged for 1992.

6.   Although Treasury Offices serve both budgets, the current system seems to assure a clear separation of the national tax administration from local government finance. Local officials interviewed during the mission expressed their satisfaction with the present administration of tax collection through the Treasury Offices. The shares of local budgets in various national taxes are determined in the Act on Revenues of Gminas and Rules of Financing. With the exceptions of the turnover tax and the tax on dividends of state-owned enterprises, all other revenues raised by national taxes are shared with local governments. According to the Local Budget Act, gminas are entitled to 5 percent of the enterprise income tax, 30 percent of the wage tax levied on the wage fund, 30 percent of the interpersonal tax, and 50 percent of the

TABLE 1

Aggregate Gmina Budgets Approved for 1991

	Zl Billion	% of Total	% of Total Public Sector Expenditures 1/	% of GDP 2/
I. REVENUES 3/				
A. Own-Source	14,836	39.4	4.6	1.7
1. Taxes	10,183	27.0	3.2	1.2
a. Property	6,312	16.7		
b. Automobile	508	1.4		
c. Agriculture	2,581	6.8		
d. Others	782	2.1		
2. Fees	2,175	5.8	0.7	0.3
a. Admin. Charges	1,745	4.7		
b. Return on assets	430	1.1		
3. Earmarked Funds (abolished)	2,091	5.6	0.6	0.2
4. Other	387	1.0	0.1	
B. Shared National Taxes	15,757	41.8	4.9	1.8
1. Enterprise Income (5%)	6,360	16.9		
2. Enterprise Wage (33%)	7,419	19.7		
3. Honoraria (30%)	752	1.9		
4. Equalization (30%)	140	0.4		
5. Small Business (50%)	1,086	2.9		
C. National Block Grants	7,092	18.8	2.2	0.8
TOTAL REVENUES	37,685	100.0	11.7	4.3
II. EXPENDITURES				
A. Current	29,456	83.4	9.1	3.3
1. Kindergartens				
a. Healthcare	1,113	3.1		
b. Education	4,970	14.1		
2. Social Assistance	2,627	7.4		
3. Housing and Related	13,071	40.0		
4. Earmarked Funds	3,558	10.1		
5. General Administration	3,330	9.4		
6. Other	787	2.2		
B. Capital	5,880	16.6	1.8	0.7
TOTAL EXPENDITURES	35,336	100.0	10.9	4.0

Notes:

1/ Estimated as total national budget expenditures (Zl 295 trillion) plus local budget expenditures net of national block grant (Zl 28 trillion) equals Zl 323 trillion total public sectore expenditures (estimated at 36.5% of GDP). Note that these figures represent estimates at the beginning of 1991.

2/ Poland's GDP for 1991 estimated at Zl 884 trillion, or about US$ 82 billion.

3/ Do not include (a) revenues from leasing and sales of gminas' property, or (b) transfers from Voivodships or Ministry of Education (about Zl 1.0 trillion) to finance tasks delegated to gminas from the national government.

SOURCE: "Informacja o zasadach kalkulowania wielkosci subwencji ogolnych dla gmin na rok 1991, sposobie ich podzialu na poszczegoine gminy craz o przewidywanych skutkach finansowych," Ministerstwo Finansow, December 1990.

"personal-small-business" income tax.[1] With the introduction of PIT, these
taxes -- except Corporate Income Tax (CIT) -- are abolished in 1992. The new
revenue sharing system gives local budgets a 15 percent share in PIT revenues
and 5 percent share in CIT revenues. Both taxes are to be collected by
Treasury Offices at the voivodship level, and distributed among gminas on an
origin basis.

7.   Financing of expenditures assigned either by law or by a special
agreement (delegation) with a Voivodship is provided by the Voivodship budget
(except for primary education, see below). The scope of extra assigned
administrative functions varies across gminas and is determined by local
government capacity and the willingness of a voivod to delegate provision of
administrative services. These transfers were not included in the MOF
estimates of gmina revenues in 1991 (Table 1). Several local government
officials complained that these transfers do no cover fully the costs of
providing delegated services, and are transferred to local budget with
significant delays.

8.   Until 1994, gminas have the option to assume responsibility for
providing elementary education (thereafter, this is expected to be a local
responsibility). In 1991, 95 of the 2,415 gminas (located in 23 voivodships)
have decided to do so. Funds, calculated on the basis of average costs per
pupil, are transferred from the budget of the Ministry of Education through
the state budget to gminas. According to the local officials interviewed, the
limited interest in exercising this option resulted from the perception that
the proposed education transfers were insufficient, as well as other
uncertainties involved in meeting a wide range of responsibilities newly
acquired by gminas.

B. The Block Grant: Its Size and Allocation

9.   The size of the total fiscal transfer budgeted for 1991 was estimated
to cover the projected gap between total local expenditures and their other
revenues, and to finance administrative functions delegated by a Voivodship
office appropriate for a given municipality. The latter, subject to
individual agreements with a voivodship, were not included in an aggregate
estimates of gminas' needs for extra resources. The Act on Local Revenues (15
December 1990) stipulates that the total transfer be a sum of (1) "funds
earmarked to cover essential current expenditures, (2) funds to cover gminas'
responsibilities in education, (3) funds earmarked for investment
expenditures, (4) equalization block grant."[2] The procedure developed by
the Ministry of Finance for the purpose of estimating the size and allocation
of fiscal transfers addressed the issues of inter-gmina equalization, the

_____

[1] This tax is paid by individuals involved in business activities but who
choose not to establish a firm. This is a common practice among craftsmen.
They fill out a "tax card" with estimates of annual costs and revenues subject
to the verification by a local treasury office. They pay their taxes in lump
sums. Thus, for instance, a locksmith working alone and/or with an assistant
would pay taxes based on estimates of his revenue capacity assessed by a local
treasury office.

[2] See "Ustawa z dnia 14 grudnia 1990 r. o dochodach gmin i zasadach ich
subwencjonowania w 1991 oraz o zmianie ustawy o samorzadzie terytorialnym,"
(The act of 14 December 1990 on gminas' revenues and principles of fiscal
transfers in 1991 and on the change of local self-government act) Dziennik
Ustaw, No. 89, Warsaw, 1990, p. 1209 (Article 11).

coverage of essential current and, separately, investment expenditures. Capital expenditures were estimated on the basis of the plan for 1990. The estimates of gmina own-source revenues did not include sale of assets and income from rents, sales and leases. The base for all other estimates were data for 1989, corrected for inflation and budget needs arising from new, substantially expanded responsibilities provided for in the Local Self-Government Act. The gap between gmina expenditures and revenues was estimated at Zl 7.1 trillion (later adjusted to Zl 7.5 trillion).

10.   Because of the Local Self-Government Act's provision that grants be allocated to gminas "on the basis of objective criteria", the Ministry of Finance (MOF) developed procedures using quantitative criteria to identify the expenditure needs and financing gap of gminas. The procedure is complex but transparent. Different criteria are used to determine four elements of the grant. They are as follows.

(a)   Essential Current Expenditures. Basic expenditure needs are estimated for the following: (i) education and child care; (ii) administration; (iii) water supply and drainage, urban transport, local roads, solid waste and heating; (iv) social assistance programs; (v) culture and arts; (vi) other sectors. Basic expenditure grant is allocated to local governments by the Minister of Finance according to preferential points formula. The formula in the 1991 Act is the same as used in the current year. Expenditure needs are proxied taking into account the population size and various characteristics of a gmina. The allocation is proportional to the number of points assigned to each gmina. The number of points depends on the population size and a complex weighing system. Gminas with special characteristics receive extra points on top of population size. The logic underlying this system is two-fold. First, it attributes greater "needs" for larger urban centers for communal services, for ecologically devastated areas, for areas with poor soil quality, and for gminas with infrastructure of national impact (e.g. ports). Second, extra points are granted to preserve nature and tourist areas. Thus, for example, an urban gmina with a population of 200,000 and a sea port is entitled to 12,500 extra points.[3]

(b)   Kindergartens and other Educational Facilities. The allocation is determined by the procedure used by the Central Government to estimate budgets of units that have been funded from the state budget.[4]

(c)   Investments. The Central Government's contribution to local capital expenditures is determined simply by the share of each gmina's planned current expenditures in the total of gmina current expenditures.

---

[3] The calculation is as follows: 10,000 due to the population size (200,000 * 0.05) and 2,500 (a flat rate) for a port. Assuming that the gmina has no other claims, its total points would be 212,500.

[4] In one of the gminas visited, kindergartens were being privatized, with vouchers for low-income children. The mission was informed that this was not an isolated case. With the transfer of administration and financing from Ministry of Education, gminas were cutting the amounts of resources spent for this purpose. See the World Bank, "Poland: Social Sectors Expenditure Review", Report No. 10158-POL, January 31, 1992, Chapter V.

(d)   Equalization. To compensate for disparities between gmina revenue
      generation and expenditure requirements, this element is determined by
      the following formula:

      $S = L*0.9(0.85B - A)$, where S = equalization allocation; L = population
      size; A = estimated gmina own-source revenues per capita; and B = the
      national average of gmina own-source revenues per capita.

      Gminas eligible for the equalization element of the block grant must have
      own-source revenues per capita more than 15 percent less than the national
      average. 1,563 gminas met this condition. About 50 percent of the total
      block grant is being allocated on this basis.

C.   Local Own-Source Revenues

11.   The share of own-source revenues in total local revenues indicates the
extent to which locally provided services are self-financing. Own-source
revenues include local taxes, fees and income from gmina-owned assets. The
most important gmina local taxes are those on property, agriculture, motor
vehicles, inheritances and gifts. Although tax rates are set by Gmina
Councils, their discretion is limited by maximum caps specified by the MOF.
The fees charged on administrative and other services are also subject to
direct central controls.

12.   The existing local tax system has several drawbacks. First, its tax
base is limited, partly because of the design of various tax instruments, and
also because of insufficient information to identify tax liabilities. The
mission's visits to gminas suggest significant potential for increasing local
tax revenues through fairly simple measures to expand the tax base through
better information systems. Second, some fees and tax rates are very low.
The administrative costs of collecting them may be greater than their
revenues. Finally, the upper limits on local tax rates and fees, set by the
MOF, restrict local fiscal autonomy and accountability. See Annex VIII for
details.

D.   Access to Capital Markets

13.   The Act on Local Self-Government grants municipalities limited borrowing
authority (Paragraph 54.1.4). The only financing sources available are bank
loans and bond issues. Short term bank loans for liquidity management cannot
exceed 5 percent of the expenditures approved for a given year (Paragraph 56).
This provision was subsequently changed. The Act on Local Government Revenues
of 14 December 1990 distinguished between current expenditure financing and
funding of expenditure "not reflected in local government revenues" (Paragraph
21.2). Loans for liquidity management are to be fully repaid within a year,
and can be up to 8 percent of planned annual expenditures in the first half
and up to 4 percent in the second half of a given year. The interest and
principal repayments of longer term loans, to finance investments, cannot
exceed 5 percent of total annual expenditures. No local government so far has
issued bonds.

14.   The overall level of indebtedness is low, and fell between December 1990
and August 1991. Data on local government indebtedness in aggregated form are
presented in Table 2. Both banks' exposure and local governments' deposits
fell in real terms between December 1990 and August 1991. The indebtedness in
real terms fell by 75.2 percent. It now represents 1.4 percent of total local

budget revenues approved for 1991, and 2.7 percent of revenues executed in
Jan. - June 1991.[5]

Table 2. <u>Debt and deposits of local governments in Banks</u>
             (in trillion of ZL)

Date	Debt	Deposits of gminas in banks	Net position
12.31.90	1.4	5.2	+ 3.8
03.30.91	0.9	6.9	+ 6.0
06.30.91	1.0	6.3	+ 5.3
07.30.91	0.9	6.0	+ 5.1
08.31.91	0.6	5.4	+ 4.8

SOURCE: "Kondycja budzetow wojewodow i budzetow samorzadowych po I polroczu
          1991 r." Central Office of Planning, Warsaw, September 1991

15.   The low level of indebtedness and the absence of bond-issuing activities
by local governments can be regarded as a very positive development. As many
observers have noted, Polish financial sector lacks managerial and technical
skills necessary to appraise creditworthiness of borrowers and to conduct more
sophisticated financial operations. In addition, the system of local finance
will be subject to significant changes for some time to come. The switch to
PIT as a major national shared tax on local revenues as well as the
introduction of VAT may produce hard to predict tensions in local finances.

_____

[5] Based on an estimate by the Ministry of Finance of executed local
revenues.

ANNEX II

LOCAL GOVERNMENT FINANCIAL MANAGEMENT

1.   This Annex presents an overall picture of local financial management in Poland. It begins with a presentation of the various types of governments and institutions involved in the provision of local public services (section A). It continues with a description of expenditures assignments between these various institutions (section B), and of tax assignments and related financing mechanisms (section C). This is followed by a discussion of some of the main issues that have to be considered by national and local decision makers (section D).[1]

A. Institutional Structure

2.   It is important to distinguish between five main types of institutions involved in the provision of local public services: (i) gminas, (ii) gmina satellites, (iii) voivodships, (iv) voivodship satellites, and (v) central ministries.

3.   First, there were 2,383 gminas transformed in 1990 into full-fledged local governments. As is the case in many other countries, gminas vary greatly. Table 1, which gives a break down of gminas by size, shows that there are small gminas (both classified as rural and as urban) and large gminas. There are about 50 gminas of more than 100,000 inhabitants, grouping almost one-third of the total Polish population.

Table 1. Distribution of Polish Gminas, by Size, 1990

Population size	Number of gminas	Population (in m.)	Population (in %)	Average Size (in 1,000)
Rural gminas	1547	14.6	38.2	9
Urban gminas				
<20,000	611	4.6	12.2	8
20,000-100,000	176	7.2	18.8	41
100,000-200,000	23	3.0	7.9	130
>200,000	19	7.1	18.6	374
Warsaw	7	1.7	4.5	243
Total	2383	38.1	100.0	16
Source: Calculated from Rocznik Statystycny 1991				

---

    [1] In this Annex, the following abbreviations are used: K = Thousands = 10^3; M = Million = 10^6; G = US billion = Polish (and European) milliard = 10^9; and Zl = Zlotys

4.   A given gmina may "have" one or several "satellites". These satellites
are enterprises specializing in one or several services. The three most
important satellites, which are to be found in most large or medium-size
cities, are (i) the transport company[2], (ii) the garbage collection company,
(iii) the housing company. These companies have existed for many years. They
used to be "gmina-controlled", but were formally owned by the State, and could
be "taken back" by a higher level of government. They are now entirely owned
by gminas.

5.   As deconcentrated units of the central government, voivodships are
engaged in the provision of centrally financed local public services, such as
health and welfare. On a per capita basis, voivodships expenditures are of the
same order of magnitude as gminas expenditures.

6.   Voivodships also control "satellites". The two most important voivodship
satellites are (i) hot water enterprises and (ii) cold water enterprises, that
were apparently found in every voivodships. In certain voivodships, there
were other satellites, such as regional transportation companies. Both cold
and hot water companies are in the process of being municipalised, that is of
being broken and handed over to gminas. In terms of relative importance, hot
water companies were heavy, and their expenditures represent as much as 40% of
voivodship direct expenditures.

7.   Voivodships also used to have "extrabudgetary funds", fed by subsidies
or specific fees. Most of them, but not all of them, have been abolished.
There remain a few funds, such as "environment funds", or "land protection
funds " or "cadastre funds", used for the specific purposes suggested by their
names. The total amount of expenditures of these funds is small and appears
to represent about 2-3% of voivodship direct expenditures.

8.   Not all central government expenditures, however, are channeled through
voivodships, and appear in voivodships budgets and accounts. A number of
important local public services are provided directly by central government
ministries, which may have voivodship branches or offices to that effect.
Education is a case in point. National roads, fire protection, police,
protection of historical buildings, unemployment compensation are also
administered directly by the central government.

9.   Figure 1 summarizes the above.

_____

     [2] This reflects the essential situation at the end of 1991. However, some
district heating enterprises were decentralized from voivodships to gminas in
1991, with more expected for 1992. Water and sanitation enterprises are
scheduled to be transferred form voivodships to gminas in 1992.

Figure 1.   Types of Institutions Involved in Service Provision in
            Poland, 1991

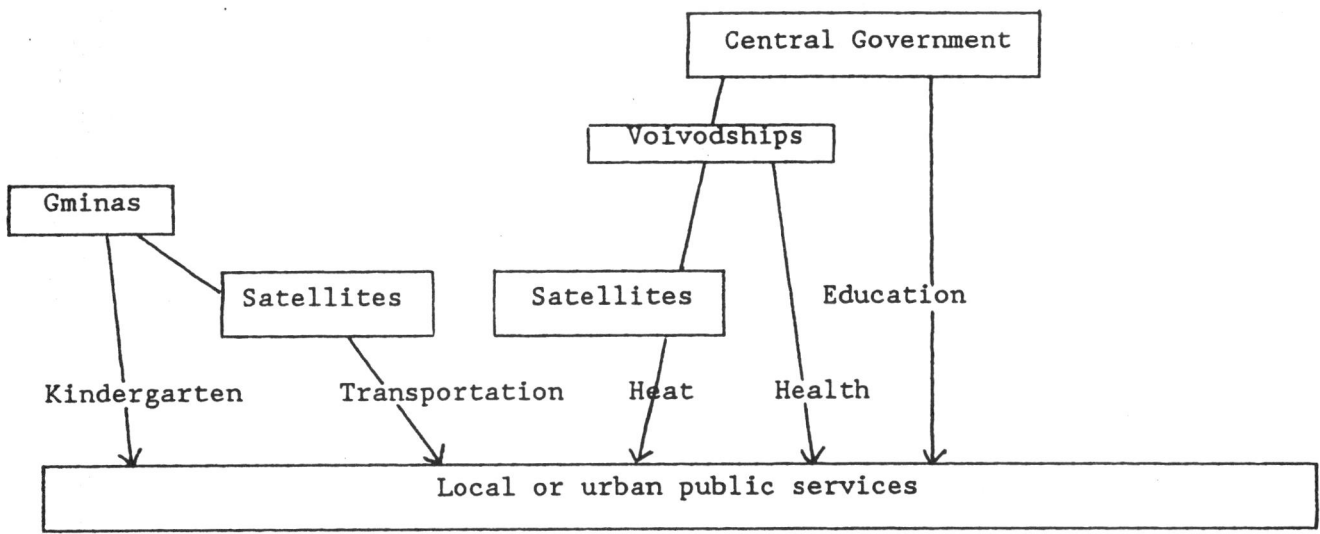

B.   Expenditure Assignment

Functional assignments

10.   The allocation of responsibilities between the various types of
institutions may be summarized in table 2, and described as follows.

11.   For education, kindergarten and pre-elementary schools are managed and
financed by gminas, where as primary, secondary, and higher education are
provided by the ministry of education (short-circuiting the voivodship).
However, it is planned that primary education, at least in terms of
investment, will become a gmina responsibility, phased in through 1994. In
1991, 95 gminas received grants for providing primary education.

12.   For transportation, several distinctions must be made. Roads and bridges
are classified into three categories. Local, or urban, roads (streets) are
allocated to gminas, regional roads to voivodships, national roads to the
ministry of transportation. Each "beneficiary" is responsible for
construction and maintenance of "its" roads. Urban bus companies are operated
by gmina satellites, at fares decided by the gmina council; urban bus
companies are heavily subsidized by gmina budgets. There seem to exist also,
at least in some voivodships, regional bus companies, for inter city
transports, which are operated by voivodship satellites. Parking, even in
cities, is a voivodship responsibility, probably because it is more associated
with the notion of traffic police than with the notion of urban public
service.

13.   Under environment, one can regroup a number of local public services.
(Cold) water supply used to be provided by voivodship satellite companies.
There was one company for each voivodship. The prices were uniform for the

whole voivodships (which implied important cross subsidies within the
voivodship). They were much higher for industry than for households (which
implied another important cross-subsidy). Sewerage was provided jointly, by
the same company. This system, however, is being dismantled. The
responsibility for the provision of cold water and sewerage is being handed
over to gminas, together with the ownership of networks. It is not clear who
will decide on the water fees. Needless to say that such a transfer is
difficult and raises delicate technical, efficiency and equity issues.

14.   The case of garbage collection and disposal is simpler. This service is
provided by gmina satellite companies, which may or may not be subsidized.
Some of these companies are also engaged in other activities, such as street
cleaning, snow cleaning, and even zoo management or gas bottles delivery. In
other cities, street cleaning is done directly by gminas. Parks creation and
management is a gmina responsibility. For certain kind of industrial wastes,
voivodships intervene with specific extra budgetary funds.

15.   For housing and related services, responsibilities are also shared. In
addition to privately owned houses and cooperatives, there are houses
belonging to enterprises, and "public houses". Public houses have been handed
over to gminas. In practice, they are owned and operated by gmina housing
satellites (called PGMs). Housing satellites also own and rent commercial
space. Rents are decided nationally, and are only a function of flat size.
They therefore bear no relationship to location: a 50 m2 flat in downtown
Warsaw is rented at the same price as a 50 m2 flat in a far away suburb in a
small provincial city. Rents for residential purposes are extremely low.
Rents for commercial purposes are much higher, thus giving rise to important
(and not well known) cross-subsidies. Nevertheless, total rents do not cover
total costs (consisting mostly of maintenance expenditures and heat
purchases), and housing companies also receive subsidies from the gmina
budgets.

16.   For heat and hot water, there is a great development of district heating
in Poland. Potentially, from a technical viewpoint, this is an energy saving
system; but in practice, for managerial reasons, it turns out to be energy
wasteful. District heating hot water is provided by voivodships satellite
companies. As was the case for water, there is one company for each
voivodships, which runs, obviously, several distinct heating systems. This
company sells, at average cost (figured out in a not very meaningful manner)
heat or hot water to industrial buildings, to cooperatives, to public housing
enterprises and even to individual houses. This implies important
cross-subsidies within each voivodships. Cooperatives and public housing
enterprises resell heat to households who are the final users. The price at
which households pay this heat is decided by the national government, and it
is not based upon effective consumption, but upon the area of the flat of the
household. The fee or price paid by household to the public housing company is
much below the price paid by the public household company to the heat
supplying company; this difference is an important cause of the deficit
incurred by public housing companies, which is covered by gminas subsidies. A
similar system operates for cooperatives. Cooperatives members pay for their
heat at the nationally decided price; cooperatives therefore incur losses,
which are covered by central government subsidies. Such a system encourages

irresponsibilities and waste. It will be changed in 1992. Heat companies will be "communalised", that is broken down and handed over to the gminas.

17.   Electricity and gas are supplied by nationwide utilities controlled by the ministry of Industry.

18.   Street lighting is supplied by gminas.

19.   For *health and welfare*, the role of gminas is not large. Health services are provided by voivodships (and constitute a major share of their expenditures). Welfare is also basically a voivodships responsibility, although gminas are also involved (with and without special subsidies from the voivodships budget), and although unemployment compensation are handled directly by a specific ministry.

20.   For *recreation*, the main role is played by gminas. They are responsible for culture, libraries, sports, theaters.

21.   For *safety*, it is the central government, not even the voivodships, which is the main actor. Police, and even fire protection, are directly supplied by central government ministries.

22.   This allocation of responsibilities between the various institutions involved in local public service provision is summed up in the following Table 2.   Additional information on the intergovernmental distribution of service delivery responsibility is provided in Annex V.

Table 2. <u>Expenditures Assignments, by service and institution, 1991</u>

	by gminas		by central government		
	Directly	Satellites	Voivodships	Satellites	Directly
Education					
Kindergarten	100				
Primary Education	4				96
Secondary					100
Higher					100
Transportation					
Local roads	100				
Regional roads			100		
National roads					100
Urban bus transport	100				
Regional bus transport				100	
Parking					100
Environment					
Water supply[a]		50		50	
Sewerage[a]		50		50	
Garbage		100			
Housing & related services					
Public housing		100			
Heat				100	
Electricity and gas					100
Street lighting	100				
Health & welfare					
Health			100		
Welfare	20		50		30
Recreation					
Culture, libraries, etc	100				
Safety					
Police					100
Fire protection					100

Notes: a(Cold) water and sewerage is being transferred from voivodship satellites to gmina satellites

Relative importance of expenditures on local public services by types of institutions

23.   How much is being spent by each of these types of institutions? Attachment A provides data on the total expenditures incurred by 15 different institutions visited by the mission. The figures given, however, are difficult to compare, because the number of people served differ widely from case to case, and also because there are subsidies given by some institutions to others. A more useful approach might be to estimate how much a given citizen receives (in the form of public services) from the various institutions. Table 3, based on the limited sample of Attachment A, provides broad estimates of such magnitudes.

Table 3.   Per Capita Expenditures on Local Public Services, by Type of Institutions, 1991.

	(in US $)	(in %)
Services provided by gminas Directly By satellites	100 60	25 15
Services provided by central government By voivodships By voivodship satellites Directly by ministries	100 40 100	25 10 25
Total	400	100
Source: Adapted from Attachment A		

24.   The meaning of table 3 is that gminas and their satellites, account for about 40% of expenditures on local public services. The share of services provided by voivodships is about similar. The balance is provided directly by central government ministries. Local public services do not include defense, justice, unemployment compensation and other services usually considered national rather than local.

Structure of gmina and voivodship expenditures

25.   The following table 4 gives a break down of expenditures of several gminas by type, for three different gminas. The first two, Kielce and Radom, are relatively large cities (214,000 people and 250,000 people, respectively), while the third one is a small urban gmina (23,500 people).

Table 4. Expenditures of Selected Gminas, by Type, 1991

	Kielce[a] (%)	Radom[b] (%)	Radom[c] (%)	Szydlowiec[d] (%)
Administration	7	4	13	
Education				
Kindergarten	14	14	19	14
Nurseries	4	2	3	-
Primary education	-	28	-	-
Road repairs	6	4	5	5
Street lighting	3	3	4	6
Parks, culture, sports	5	2	3	6
Welfare	2	1	2	6
Subsidies to satellites				
Public transport sat.	14	8	12	
Housing satellite	8	8	11	10
Garbage satellite	4	3	4	2
Infrastructure investments	28[e]	10[f]	14[f]	4[g]
Other	6	12	17	34[h]
Total	100	100	100	100
Total (in Gz)	247	348	251	11

Notes: [a]Execured budget for Jan-Nov. (11 months); [b]Planned & including primary education expenditures financed by a special grant from the ministry of finance; [c]Planned, but excluding this primary education expenditures; [d]Executed for 9 months; [e]Mostly water supply and roads; [f]Excluding expenditures on road repairs financed by a specific grant from the voivodship; [g]To be substantially increased in the last quarter of the year; [h]Including 3.3 Gz (30% of total) as reimbursement of debt.

26.   The expenditure structures of these three gminas are rather similar (when specificities are taken into account). The three most important types of expenditures are (a) subsidies to gmina satellites, (b) infrastructure investments, and (c) expenditures on kindergarten.

27.   Table 5 provides a break down of expenditures by types for two voivodships of average importance: Kielce (1,127,000 inhabitants) and Radom (750,000 inhabitants).

Table 5. Expenditures of Selected Voivodships, by Type, 1991[a]

	Kielce		Radom	
	(Gzl)	(%)	(Gzl)	(%)
Health	734	61	454	56
Welfare	138[b]	12	92[c]	11
Administration	53[d]	4	42[e]	5
Agriculture & Forestry	74	6	52[f]	6
Transportation	41	3	23	3
Culture, art, sport	32	3	23	3
Roads ("communal economy")	52[g]	4	47[h]	6
Housing economy	34	3	35	4
Subsidies to gminas	18	2	28	3
Other	19	2	17	2
Total	1195	100	813	100

Notes: [a]Planned; [b]Including 58 Gzl of subsidies to gminas for tasks undertaken by gminas on behalf of the voivodship; [c]Including 35 Gzl for the same purpose; [d]Including 12 Gzl for the same purpose; [e]Including 9 Gzl for the same purpose; [f]Including 11 Gzl for the same purpose; [g]Including 6 Gzl forthesame purpose; [h]Including 11 Gzl for the same purpose.

28.   The structure of expenditures of the two voivodships are very similar. This is not surprising. The budgets of voivodships are not decided at the voivodships level. Rather, they are decided by the central government and the Parliament. The Polish budget takes the form of a matrix, with ministries and types of expenditures in lines, and voivodships in columns, although, for some lines (corresponding to the expenditures directly undertaken by ministries) there is no pre-allocation by voivodships.

29.   The striking feature of voivodships expenditures is the predominance of health expenditures, which accounts for about 60% of total expenditures. Welfare is the second most important type of expenditures. The other types (agriculture, transportation) are of necessity relatively less important.

30.   For certain functions, such as welfare and roads, voivodships act (in part) indirectly. They subsidize gminas, which spend money on their behalf. In our two examples, subsidies to gminas account for about 2% of voivodships expenditures.

C. Tax Assignment and Related Financing Mechanisms

Tax assignment

31. The Polish tax system, and the allocation of tax proceeds to local various institutions, are changing rapidly. Until 1990, there were five main taxes (all paid by enterprises) and a few minor taxes. The main taxes were (i) the turnover tax, (ii) the so-called "dividend", which was a tax based on the capital of state-owned enterprises, (iii) a wage tax, assessed on wages paid, (iv) a wage levy, also assessed on wages, and (v) a corporate income tax based on the profits of all enterprises. The minor taxes were (i) a real estate tax, assessed on built and unbuilt property, (ii) a so-called road tax, assessed on automobile ownership, (iii) a personal income tax, levied on individuals with high income. A basic characteristic of the system was that different types of enterprises would pay different types of taxes, or pay to different kinds of institutions; thus, a central government controlled enterprise would pay its turnover tax to the central government, where as a voivodships controlled enterprise would pay it to the voivodships; or, to take another example, a state-owned enterprise would pay the wage tax but a private enterprise would be exempt.

32. This characteristic has been abolished. All enterprises are now subject to the same tax system. The main taxes, however, remained in force in 1991, and one can still identify the eight taxes mentioned above.

33. Table 6 indicates the allocation of the various Polish taxes between the two levels of government.

Table 6. Tax Assignment, 1991

	To central government	To gminas
Central government taxes		
Turnover tax	100	–
Tax on capital of publicly-owned enterprises[a]	100	100
Shared taxes		
Corporate income tax	95	5
Wage tax[c]	70	30
Personal income tax[d]	70	30
Small business income tax[c]	50	50
Local taxes		
Real estate tax	–	100
Road (auto) tax	–	100
Tax on small businesses	–	100
Agricultural tax	–	100

Notes: [a]This tax, also called "dividend", and which could be considered as property income, is levied by gminas on their own enterprises, and by the center on its own enterprises; [c]To be abolished in 1992; [d]To be transformed into a more effective personal income tax in 1992, and shared according to a 85%-15% ratio.

34. Both the present system and the system envisaged for 1992 give a great importance to shared taxes. With the exception of the turnover tax (to be transformed into a value added tax), all the important taxes are shared

between the two levels of government. Shared taxes are not very widespread in the world: Germany (where the personal income tax is shared between the three levels of government) and Brazil are significant exceptions. There is a debate about the nature of the local government share of a shared tax. Many people do not consider it as a "local tax", but as a subsidy. The argument is that it is not a local tax because the tax base, and more importantly the tax rate, completely escape the control of the local government. It can be seen as a central to local government subsidy, the total amount of which is determined as a share of the proceeds of a national tax, and which is allocated to the various local governments prorata the amount contributed from their territory,a criterion like any other criterion, and not necessarily a very good one.

35.   Table 7 indicates the amounts of taxes collected by gminas from the various own and shared taxes.

Table 7. Tax Revenues, by Type, Selected Gminas, 1991

	Kielce[a]	Radom[b]	Szydloviec[b]
Own taxes			
Property tax	38.0	40.0	3.1
Auto tax	3.5	2.0	c
Tax on small businesses	4.7	4.0	c
Agricultural taxes	0.3	0.9	c
Total own taxes	46.5	46.9	3.1[d]
Shared taxes			
Corporate income tax (5%)	60.0	21.9	0.4
Wages taxes (30%)	65.8	58.2	5.4
Personal income tax (30%)	-	1.2	-
Small business income tax (50%)	5.6	21.0	0.3
Total shared taxes	131.4	102.3	6.1
Total taxes	177.9	149.2	9.2

Notes: [a]Executed budget for 11 months; [b]Planned; [c]Unidentified; [d]Excluding auto tax and tax on small business

36.   Several points can be made about local and shared taxation. First, at this stage, the revenue importance of the shared taxes is about twice as large as that of own taxes; in other words own taxes account for about one-third of total taxes.

37.   Second, own taxes consist mainly (about 80%) of the property tax, which is a tax on the ownership of land and buildings, assessed on surface rather than on value. The other local taxes are the automobile tax (also called road tax), a tax assessed on vehicle ownership (which is a form of property tax), and a tax on small businesses. The rates of these taxes are set by gminas, within ceilings imposed by the Ministry of Finance.

38.   Third, the most important shared taxes are taxes on wages, and on corporate income. The rates of these taxes are decided nationally, just as the exact tax bases (the definition of corporate income is conventional), and each gmina get 30% and 5%, respectively, of the proceeds of the taxes paid in its

jurisdiction. These taxes are paid by all enterprises, but, as state-owned enterprise still account for the bulk of enterprises in Poland, and there fore of wages paid, and even of profits made, these taxes are mostly contributed by state-owned enterprises.

39.   Fourth, in 1991, own taxes fared better than shared taxes. The evidence (not shown in table 7) is that the property tax collected generally achieved or exceeded budgeted targets, whereas wages taxes, and above all corporate income tax, often fell short of planned figures, by as much as 50% in some cases.   The reason is that a number of state-owned enterprises are making losses rather than profits, and that some of them are laying off workers, therefore reducing wages paid. In other words, the tax bases of the main shared taxes are shrinking. This is a dramatic problem for the national budget, but also for the gmina budgets. By contrast, the tax base of the gmina property tax remained constant, and households and enterprises paid the tax assessed on it at reasonable rates, although it is reported that some state-owned enterprises in a particularly bad shape were not paying their property taxes.

Other resources of gminas

40.   In Poland, as elsewhere, gminas are not financed only by taxation. Table 8 indicates, for selected gminas, the structure of their resources. For Radom, there are two sets of figures. One includes a very large grant given for the construction of a primary school; the other excludes this grant, which is not standard, and therefore not representative of gmina resources.

41.   Table 8 also presents the structure of resources in two ways. First shared taxes are considered as taxes. Second, shared taxes are considered as grants.

Table 8.   Structure of Resources, Selected Gminas, 1991

	Kielce[a]	Radom[b][c]	Radom[b][d]	Szydloviec[b]
A - Considering shared taxes as taxes				
Taxes (own & shared taxes)	72	39	52	45
Grants	7	37	15	28
Property income, fees, etc	28	23	31	29
Total	100	100	100	100
B - Considering shared taxes as grants				
Taxes (own taxes only)	19	12	16	15
Granted (shared taxes & grants)	60	64	51	58
Property income, fees, etc.	28	23	31	29
Total	100	100	100	100

Source: Attachment B
Notes: [a]Executed for 11 months; [b]Planned: [c]Including a 97Gzl grant for the construction of a primary school; [d]Excluding this grant

42.   Table 8 shows the importance of grants, and correlatively gives an indication of the degree of fiscal autonomy of local governments in Poland. If one considers shared taxes as grants, on the basis that gminas have no control whatsoever on the amount of shared taxes they receive, then it appears that gminas receive about half of their resources from the central government, in the form of shared taxes and grants.

43.   Grants and subsidies can be classified into several categories. In addition to the shared taxes, a distinction must be made between a block grant and specific grants. A block grant is given to all gminas by the Ministry of Finance, according to a complex formula. There are three main components or elements to the block grant: (i) a *needs* element, which amounted to about 40% of the total in 1991, (ii) an *equalization* element, which amounted to about 59%, and (iii) an *investment* element, for about 10%. The "needs" element takes population into consideration, but gives additional money for special needs, such as those associated with the existence of a national infrastructure (e.g. a port), or with degraded environmental conditions. The equalization element compensates partially differences in estimated own source revenues of gminas, according to the following formula:

$$E = P*0.9(0.85B - A)$$

with E = the amount of the equalization element received by a given gmina, P = the population of this gmina, B = the estimated per capita own-revenue resources of the gmina, A = the average estimated per capita own-resources of all Polish gminas. The investment element is determined as a function of the share of planned investment expenditures in total planned expenditures.

44.   A fourth element, relative to *education, is* often presented as being a component of the allocation formula. About 95 gminas (such as Radom) took over primary education, signed contracts to that effect with the Ministry of Finance, and receive grants for that purpose. But these grants are ear-marked for primary education, and should better be considered as specific grants.

45.   Gminas also benefit from specific grants. As mentioned above, education grants by the Ministry of Finance should be considered as such. Gminas also receive subsidies from voivodships, that are ear-marked for specific purposes, such as road construction or welfare.

46.   The balance of gmina resources come from property income and fees (and also from a surplus from the previous year). Attachment B gives figures for these resources for selected gminas. Three particular types of resources call from some comments. First, gminas levy on the enterprises they own a so-called "dividend", assessed on the capital of these enterprises. This dividend is often considered as a tax, but it can equally be seen as property income. Second, there are rents,

collected by gminas from the tenants of industrial or commercial
properties owned by gminas. Third, there are, for some gminas at least,
the proceeds of the sales of gmina properties. In addition to such
property income, which is not negligible (it amounts to more than 10% of
total income in the gminas for which this detailed information was
obtained), there are fees on transactions. Such fees can be considered as
the payment for a specific service (the registration and the
certification of the transaction) but also as a tax levied on
transactions.

Financing mechanisms

47.   Figure 2 gives a simplified picture of the financial flows involved
in the provision of local public services in Poland.

Figure 2.   Financing Mechanisms

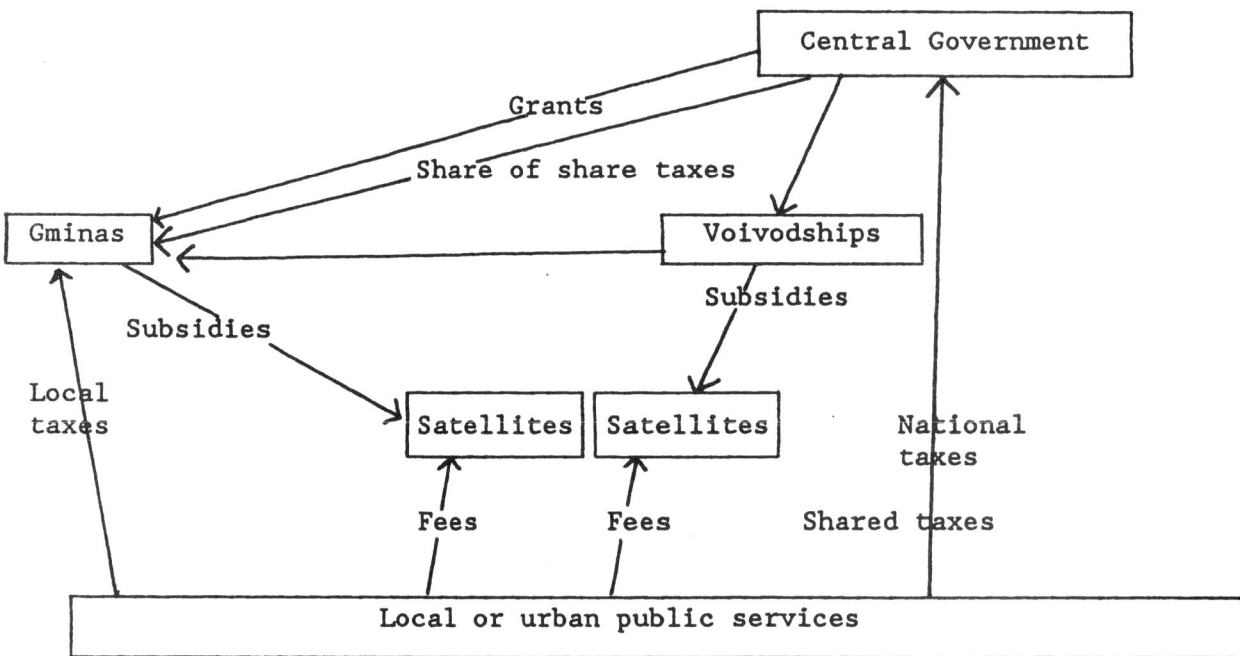

48.   Figure 2 shows clearly the key role of the Ministry of Finance. In
the framework set by law it decides on the amount and allocation of
subsidies to gminas, on the shares of shared taxes allocated to gminas,
on the amount and on the structure of voivodships budgets, and on the
amounts given to the various ministries for direct spending outside
voivodships budgets.

49.   Figure 2 also shows the role of satellites. An examination of the
accounts of housing satellites for several cities, presented in Table 9,
may throw some light on this role.

Table 9.   Income and Expenditures of Housing Satellites, Selected
            Cities, 1990 & 1991

	Warsaw[a] (Gzl)	Kielce[b] (Gzl)	Radom[c] (Gzl)
Income			
Rents	6	25	31
Fees for water, heat, garbage	6	d	d
Subsidy from gmina	33	9[e]	34[f]
Total, income	45	34	65
Expenditures			
Heat	16	11	23
Maintenance	17	23	16
Cold water & garbage	3	d	11
Administration	6[g]	d	6
Total, expenditures	45	34	56[h]

Notes: [a]PGM Warszawa Stare Miasto, renting about 10,000 flats (437,000 m2) and 500 commercial premises (80,000 m2), for 1990; [b]PGM Kielce, renting about 20,000 flats (520,000 m2) and commercial premises (70,000 m2), for the 9 first months of 1991; [c]PGM Radom, for the 10 first months of 1991; [d]Included in the figure above; [e]Differs from figure in Table 4, possibly because periods considered are different; [f]Differs from figure in Table 4, possibly because it refers to actual as opposed to planned expenditures; [g]Including a "profit" of 3 Gzl; [h]Differs from figure given for total income, for unknown reasons

50.   Although the figures differ markedly from case to case, and are not always very convincing, Table 9 serves to illustrate the economy of public housing, and the financial mechanisms utilized. First, expenditures seriously underestimate costs. The cost of capital (interest and capital repayment in case of loan financing), which is the most important component of housing costs, is completely ignored. Depreciation is also ignored, and cannot be supposed to be equal to maintenance expenditures. Second, heat expenditures are very high, and represent about one third of total recorded expenditures; yet these heat expenditures are paid to the voivodships satellite, at prices which are already lowered by important coal subsidies, and do not represent the true cost of heat consumed. Third, rents and fees paid by tenants cover only a fraction (one fourth to three fourths, in our examples) of the expenditures incurred by the housing satellite. Four, although this does not appear in Table 9, house holds pay in rents and fees relatively much less than enterprises renting commercial premises.

51.   Households fortunate enough to have access to public housing are therefore subsidized by at least four mechanisms. They are cross-subsidized by commercial premises, and, beyond, by consumers. They are also subsidized by coal subsidies. They are further subsidized by society at large, which financed housing construction. They are finally subsidized by gminas, that give important subsidies to housing satellites. Furthermore, some house holds are more subsidized than others; they all pay much less than costs, but some pay even less than other, since the rents and fees paid bear no relationship to location, which nevertheless influences costs.

D. Issues

52.   This evolving system of local public services provision raises a
number of issues, that can be discussed under the three headings of (i)
State administration, (ii) taxes and grants, (iii) local policies. The
issues of taxes and grants and of gmina policies are of concern to both
the central and local governments.

State administration

53.   The present Polish system of government and administration is a
two-tier system: public services are provided by a central government and
by over 2,400 gminas. Should a third tier be introduced? If so, what
should it be? There are many people who advocate the creation of an
intermediate level of government, which could be either the existing 49
voivodships, or a larger number of regions, often called powiats. They
argue that voivodships are a relatively new creation in Poland (they were
introduced in the early 1970ies), and that powiats have existed both
before and after the war. They also argue that voivodships are not of the
appropriate design and size for many functions.

54.   This discussion confuses two distinct issues. One is the issue of
further decentralization, of creating an additional tier of government
(which would or would not follow the design of existing voivodships). The
other is the issue of different design, of restructuring the map of
Poland (with or without decentralization). There are therefore four
options under discussion: (i) the status quo, (ii) the creation of a new
design without a new level of government, (iii) the creation of a new
level of government within the existing design, and (iv) the creation of
a new level of government together with a new design.

55.   Creating an additional level of government is probably a good idea.
Most countries of Western Europe (with the exception of the United
Kingdom) have three, or even four, tiers of government.[3] An
intermediate level would be useful. The real issue here is whether this
creation is urgent and should take place in the immediate future. The
answer is most probably negative. Poland has just introduced a measure of
decentralization by transforming gminas into full- fledged local
governments, by assigning functions and taxes to this new tier of
government. It will take some years to digest this important reform.
Further decentralization at this stage would create confusion, generate
additional costs, require more political and administrative personnel
(already in short supply). It could weaken gminas, which need to be
strengthened. This seems to eliminate options (iii) and (iv), at least
for some years to come.

---

[3] See Annex IV for additional information on Polish local government in
international perspective.

56.   Redesigning the administrative map of Poland (option (ii)) is a different proposition. It is true that many countries, particularly in Western Europe, are divided into regions which are much larger than Polish voivodships. It is also argued that larger administrative circumscriptions would be a return to pre 1970 traditions, and more effective for economic and social management.

57.   None of these arguments is very convincing. Countries divided into large regions are often also further divided into smaller units (France is divided into departments as well as into regions; Germany in kreis as well as in lander, Italy in provinces as well as in regions, etc.) History, in a matter like this, and in a country which has changed so much, has not much normative significance. As for the third argument, it is most probably true that the territorial design of voivodships is not ideal for the provision of certain services such as, let us say, health or regional roads. But the same will be equally true of *any* territorial design. The one that would be good for health and roads would not be good for fire protection and power provision. The idea that there is *one* perfect territorial design is but a myth. All territorial designs are imperfect.

58.   The present one seems quite workable. Existing voivodships are not too dissimilar in size (unlike what is often found in certain countries). Each of them is centered on a major city, and is named after that city. As a matter of fact, voivodships are very similar in both population and area to the French departments. The French departments have often been criticized, but for about two centuries they have been utilized as the basic unit of administration of the French State.

59.   Even if it could be shown that another design would be "better" -which does not seem to be the case- this would not mean that this new design must be adopted, or at least must be adopted now. The benefits of the change would have to be weighted against the costs of the change. Creating new circumscriptions, particularly if they were not the mere addition of existing voivodships, would be costly and traumatic. Valuable information and procedures would be lost. As this stage, Poland has so much to do with the many shocks and changes of the structural megadjustment in process that it should seek to avoid all the shocks and changes that are not absolutely necessary.

60.   A more immediate issue might be that of the role of the voivod. The voivod is the representative of the central government in every part of the country. Yet, his powers are rather limited. First, as we have seen, entire central government functions (such as education or police) are performed directly by ministries and their own representatives over whom he has no control. Second, for the functions which are under his responsibility (and appear as expenditures in his budget), he receives detailed orders from Warsaw and has practically no control over his budget. He is in part by-passed, and in part constrained. Only with the extra budgetary funds, which are supposed to be phased out, has he a fair degree of discretion. It would seem that the means at the disposal of the voivoid are not commensurate with his responsibilities. The possibility

to strengthen the role of the voivoid should be studied. The distinction between direct ministry expenditures and voivodships expenditures could be revised. It would be desirable to regroup all central government expenditures in one single budget, and to give the voivoid some control over all these expenditures. It would also be desirable to give him some discretion in the functional allocation of expenditures, e.g. to introduce some form of deconcentration. A balance must be found between the need to give ministries and their local representatives the means to conduct national sectorial policies, and the need to give voivods the possibility to develop local global policies. It is important to note, in this respect, that deconcentration (more powers to voivods) is, to a certain extent, an alternative to decentralization (more powers to locally elected councils). If it is decided, as seems reasonable, not to decentralize further in the near term, then it is all the more desirable to deconcentrate and to strengthen the voivods.

61.   Another, different, area, in which the central government should take initiative is the budgeting and accounting procedures of voivodships and of gminas. At present, budgets and accounts are presented in ways that do not lend themselves to analysis, and to rational decision making. The form utilized by the ministry of Finance to collect information about gmina budgets, for instance, include an item entitled "other income". This item is usually very large, and it regroups sources of income which are completely different: some are local taxes (like the automobile tax), other are sales of local properties, yet other surplus from the previous year. The 14-item nomenclature utilized by gminas to record expenditures has an item (number 74) entitled "communal economy" that regroups most of their tasks: from street lighting to parks to subsidies to gmina satellites, and therefore a disproportionate share of gmina expenditures. What is needed are meaningful nomenclatures that will make it possible for gminas to effectively plan their expenditures, and for the analysts, including the central government, to understand and monitor gmina expenditures. Such nomenclatures must of course be provided, and imposed, by the central government, for purposes of comparison and of aggregation; otherwise, if every gmina were to devise its own system, such comparison and aggregation would become impossible.

Taxes and grants

62.   Gminas play an important role in the provision of local public services, and their output is in part conditioned by their resources, and, in particular by taxes and grants, which constitute the bulk of their resources.

63.   Gminas are not much favored in the existing allocation of taxes. They are endowed with an antiquated property tax, an automobile tax, and a tax on small businesses. Under current constraints, they have done reasonably well with "their" taxes, and taxes collected have in many cases exceeded forecasts. The property tax is theoretically a good local tax, probably the best local tax, mostly because property, particularly land, cannot easily be moved out of the taxing jurisdiction, and also because its burden is often considered progressive or at least

proportional (although there are divergent views on this matter). On the other hand, property taxes are difficult to administer, and for this reason unfit for some low income countries that do not have the required administrative capacity. This, however, would not be the case of Poland. A long tradition of intellectual achievement, reinforced by forty years of central planning (a heavy consumer of data and information) makes it possible for Poland to develop a sophisticated and efficient property tax. The most important change to be introduced is to base the tax on the market value of properties, and not on the surface of properties. An improvement of the titles registration system, which is also needed for other purposes (to facilitate security of tenure, and mobility, and the development of a mortgage market) is another ingredient of the necessary reform. Strengthening property tax administration in Poland is clearly a priority task, and one that could be greatly facilitated by international assistance. Specific recommendations are presented in Annex VI, Section D, and Annex VIII.

64.   The other local taxes (automobile tax, tax on small businesses) have at present very low yields. It is desirable that there be more than one local tax, and automobile ownership as well as business activity are suitable bases for local taxation. Additional work is required to study the potential and the administration of these taxes, and of other taxes.

65.   If one considers shared taxes as grants, then it can be said that grants constitute a very large share of gmina resources. This share is probably too large, especially in local government accountability is to be emphasized. Also important, the structure of grants is not appropriate.

66.   The bulk of grants are shared taxes, and these shared taxes have three major draw backs: (i) they are uncertain, (ii) they are threatened, and in any case (iii) they are unfair. The taxes shared so far were in practice taxes on enterprises, based on wages and on profits. In the present Polish economic circumstances, such taxes bases are extremely uncertain. Profit, in particular, constitutes a very volatile base. Many enterprises, particularly state-owned enterprises have a zero or a negative profit. This is reflected in the figures relative to taxes collected in 1991, which are often very different (usually inferior) from budgeted figures. For a given gmina, the proceeds of shared taxes resembles more a lottery than a stable source of income.

67.   Even if the proceeds of shared taxes were satisfactory, shared taxes would still have a weakness. They are unfair. They favor those gminas where tax bases are located, which are usually also the gminas with the greatest local taxation potential, and not necessarily the gminas with a tax base insufficient to discharge responsibilities assigned to them. More is given to the richer gminas, in terms of activity, income, own tax resources. When uncorrected, shared taxes increase intergmina disparities. In a country like Germany, which relies heavily on shared taxes for both lander and local governments income, this system is accompanied and corrected by a complex equalization mechanism (finanzausgleicht). It is true that the Polish block grant

allocation formula has also an "equalization element", which is a first
step in this direction. But the magnitudes involved are such that it is
very difficult to believe that disparities are fully corrected. At best,
the block grant diminishes the disparities created by the shared taxes
grants. Taken altogether, the Polish grants probably increase intergmina
disparities.

68.   Regarding the block grant, determination of the total amount is not
clear. There are, generally speaking, two types of block grants with
respect to the total amount granted. There are "closed" systems, in
which a total amount is first decided (for instance as equal to a share
of a certain national tax, or of certain national taxes, as in France or
in Korea), then allocated amongst local governments by means of an
allocation formula. There are also, much less frequently, "open "
systems, in which formulas determine the amount received by each local
government, the total granted resulting from the sum of these individual
amounts. The Polish system seems to borrow features from both types of
grants. The design of the equalization element implies an "open" system;
the design of the "needs" element (which determines "points" for each
gmina) suggests a "closed" system. In practice, the ministry of Finance
utilizes what it calls a "macro-budget" for all gminas, and defines total
grants as the difference between expenditures and income, with
expenditures defined on the basis of past expenditures, and income
estimated in an unspecified fashion. This appears to create serious
discussions for local resource mobilization. It would probably be
clearer, and better understood by gminas, if a simpler closed model were
adopted, that would distinguish between the determination of the total
amount of grants, and then the allocation of this total amongst the 2,400
gminas.

69.   Such a procedure, however, would be in conflict with the present
practice of not necessarily distributing the total amount of block grant,
another complicating feature of the existing system. In 1991, the grant
was distributed monthly. Every month, each gmina would receive
one-twelfth of what it was entitled to for the entire year. The system
worked well for the first 9 months of the year. In October, however, for
macro-economic reasons, the ministry of Finance decided to reduce the
grants payment. Overall, gminas will receive about 90% of the planned
grant. The cuts were not homothetical. Some gminas were spared,
according to complex, but not discretionary, formulas. The net result is
that there is a degree of uncertainty in grants: gminas cannot count on a
predetermined amount of grant for a given year. It is easy to understand
that, in a difficult macro-economic situation, the ministry of Finance
hesitates to tie its hands, and wants to retain some flexibility.
Nevertheless, local governments also need to know what their resources
will be if they are to spend in a responsible and efficient manner. A
compromise should be sought.

70.   In summary, given Poland's extreme macroeconomic constraints, the
preferred general strategy would be to clearly define gminas expenditures
responsibilities, encourage local cost recovery and tax mobilization,
reduce or eliminate local dependance on shared taxes and emphasize the

equalization role of block grants, with these grants determined in an amount consistent with the macroeconomic adjustment program and then provide assurances to gminas that their block allocations will be provided in an effective and timely manner.

Local policies

71.   Local governments operate under difficult conditions. Their resources are not predictable, their experience limited, and their tasks immense. There is a general consensus that, on the whole, gminas elected councils and mayors have done rather well. They seem to have learned quickly, and their performances in 1991, their second year, are reported to show improvement over their performance in 1990, their first year. They face three main issues.

72.   One has to do with planning and budgeting. It is apparent that the system as it functions now makes it extremely difficult, if not impossible, for gminas to plan and to budget. Figuring out the yield of shared taxes is more like guessing than forecasting, and will be even more so with the new taxes introduced. The amount of the block grant is decided and communicated well after the beginning of the year, and may be cut before the end of the year, so that choosing a figure for this item in a budget is a form of art. Estimating the yield of the property tax is probably easier, although rates are capped and allowance must be made for enterprises that will be unwilling to pay. There are also uncertainties on the expenditures side, such as those which are associated with nationally set prices for housing, fuels, heat, that determine the amount of subsidies given to gmina satellites. In addition, as mentioned above, the accounting frame work utilized (and prepared by the central government) does not lend itself to analysis and forecasting. To make matters more complicated, high inflation rates lessen the significance and usefulness of budgets (whether a given income or expenditure takes place at the beginning or at the end of the year matters). As a result, it is difficult for budgets to play the policy role and the control role which they should normally play.

73.   A second policy issue is debt financing. The information collected on the indebtedness of gminas is mixed. On the one hand it was reported that about 900 gminas (nearly 40% of all gminas), including many large cities, are in debt. It seems that in 1990, many gminas borrowed from banks. On the other hand, it was reported that gminas are not allowed to borrow more than 5% of their current budgeted expenditures. In general, it can be said that debt financing is reasonable, and that the problem is more a problem of who should lend, at what rates, and against what guarantees, than a problem of principle.

74.   The third local policy issue is that of the management of gmina properties, including their satellites, and particularly their housing satellites. It raises delicate problems of privatization, of management, of pricing. Gminas happen to be the owners of a number of properties, such as land, houses, factories, buildings, satellites (and they are now being given water and heat satellites created out of water and heat voivodships' satellites companies), etc. A distinction must be made between "ordinary" and "social" properties.

75.   "Ordinary" properties are enterprises engaged in the production of private goods. In most other countries, such enterprises are owned by private investors. Polish gminas have inherited some properties of that type. In Radom, there are 5 such enterprises, including a construction company, employing about 1,200 workers. In Kielce, several enterprises, including a fashion company, employ nearly 5,000 workers.

76.   "Social" properties are enterprises engaged in the production of public or semi-public goods and services, such as garbage collection or public transportation. These enterprises often take the form of regulated utilities in most other countries. In Poland, they normally take the form of satellites.

77.   Many gminas do not know what to do with their "ordinary" properties. Either they loose money, and gminas hesitate to sell enterprises that have a low value; or they make money, and gminas also hesitate to sell them and loose a source of income. At a time when unemployment is growing, elected councils are also very reluctant to dispose of enterprises that do employ workers. Some gminas even consider investing in "ordinary" enterprises, or in banks, in order to "create jobs", and to "influence economic development". They should be warned about the dangers of such actions. Managing an ordinary enterprise, or a bank, is a difficult, specialized and full-time job, that will be better done by private entrepreneurs than by elected politicians. Councils and mayors will be slow to take decisions, unaware of business opportunities, worried about the political impacts of their decisions, and are unlikely to be successful businessmen. And the time they will devote to "their" enterprises will not be devoted to the equally difficult, specialized and full time of managing a city.

78.   The case of "social" properties is quite different. The system of garbage, water, transport and heat satellites is not necessarily bad. Some of the services they perform should not be rendered by the market alone, and some form of public decision or supervision may be necessary.

79.   The Polish experience provides positive examples. The head of a satellite is potentially under pressure to "deliver", and to do so at a reasonable cost, because the subsidy he receives is visible and in many cases should disappear. This pressure, however, has not always been sufficient, and it seems that the "cost plus" system which has prevailed (the difference between costs and fees was automatically covered by a subsidy) has discouraged efficiency. The problem is that these satellites are in a monopoly position, and that like all monopolies, they tend to

take advantage of their situation.

80.   An option, which might be considered is the development of "concessions". Under this arrangement, a local government contracts with a private company for the provision in its jurisdiction of a certain local public service such as water supply or garbage collection. The contract stipulates the technical and locational characteristics of the service, as well as the prices to be charged. It is a long- term contract, and during the concession period, the concessionnaire also enjoys a monopoly. But competition intervenes at the time of renewing the concession, because several companies can and will bid for it, and therefore introduces the pressure of competition in the system. Such a system is widely utilized in a country like France. It could be considered by Poland, and existence of satellites would facilitate its introduction. Significant technical assistance would be required, however, for gminas to effectively design and manage a competitive bidding negotiations, contracting and supervision system (see Section D, Annex VI).

81.   Another issue associated with the management of "social" enterprises is pricing. So far, the prices of water, sewage, heat, housing (rents), garbage collection, etc. paid by households and enterprises partly or totally escaped gminas. This will be less and less so. Gminas will have to make difficult and interrelated decisions, for which they are not generally well prepared. Some guidelines can be formulated. Including a better understanding of costs, both financial and economic as prerequisite to pricing.

82.   In the case of gmina residential and commercial buildings, there is also the option of selling. For housing, this may not be attractive at present, because rental housing is so heavily subsidized: few people want to buy what they get for free (or for a nominal charge). But as public housing rents increase, the tenants will be more induced to buy, and gminas to sell.

EXPENDITURES BY TYPES OF INSTITUTIONS

Table A-1. Expenditures on Local Public services, Selected Institutions, 1991

	Total Expenditures (Gz)	Population (1,000)	Exp./cap. (Mz)	Exp./cap. (US$)
Gmina expenditures:				
Krakow	1178	750	1.57	143
Kielce[a]	247	214	1.15	105
Maslow	6.5	8	0.81	74
Radom[b]	377	250	1.51	137
Radom[c]	280	250	1.12	102
Szydlowiec[d]	20.4	23.5	0.86	78
Gmina satellites expenditures:				
Housing, Kielce	33	214	0.15	14
Transportation, Kielce	78	250[e]	0.31	28
Garbage, Kielce	11	214	0.05	5
Transport, Radom	64	280[e]	0.23	21
Garbage, Radom[f]	40	280[e]	0.14	13
Voivodship expenditures:				
Kielce	1195	1126	1.07	97
Radom	814	750	1.08	98
Voivodship satellites expenditures:				
Heat, Radom	300	750	0.40	36
Direct central Government expenditures:				
Education, Kielce	431	750	0.57	52
Education, Katowice	3040	3980	0.76	69

Sources: field visits. Notes: [a]Executed budget for January-November; [b]Including 97 Gz for primary education, financed by a specific grant; [c]Excluding these 97 Gz [d]Planned expenditures; [e]Gross estimates; these satellites also serve adjacent smaller gminas; [f]Including a zoo, parks, gas bottles.

INCOME OF GMINAS

Table B-1. Resources of Selected Gminas, 1991

	Kielce[a] (Gzl)	Radom[b] (Gzl)	Szydloviec[b] (Gzl)
Own taxes			
Property tax	38.0	40.0	3.1
Auto tax	3.5	2.0	c
Tax on small businesses	4.7	4.0	c
Agricultural taxes	0.3	0.9	c
Total own taxes	46.5	46.9	3.1[d]
Shared taxes			
Corporate income tax (5%)	60.0	21.9	0.4
Wages taxes (30%)	65.8	58.2	5.4
Personal income tax (30%)	-	1.2	-
Small business income tax (50%)	5.6	21.0	0.3
Total shared taxes	131.4	102.3	6.1
Grants & Subsidies			
Block grant	13.2	14.3	4.6
Specific grants	3.2	126.8[e]	1.1
Total grants	16.2	141.1	5.7
Property income, fees, miscellaneous			
Surplus from previous year	16.0	23.0	c
Capital tax on gmina enterprises[g]	5.6	4.0	c
Rents	18.0	21.0	c
Sale of property	-	12.0	c
Other (mostly fees[h])	14.3	27.0	c
Total, property income, etc.	53.9	87.2	6.0
Total	248.1	377.5	20.4

Notes: [a]Executed budget for 11 months; [b]Planned; [c]Unidentified; [d]Excluding auto tax and tax on small business; [e]Including 97 Gzl from the ministry of finance for the construction of a primary school, and 29.8 from the voivodship for specific purposes; [f]From the voivodship for specific purposes; [g]Called "dividend, and often considered as a tax; [h]Including a fee on transactions, which could also be considered as a tax on transactions

ANNEX III

REVIEW OF BUDGET EXECUTION FOR A SAMPLE OF GMINAS

1.   Local governments now operate under a new financial system that was
introduced in January 1991 (see Annexes I and II). Local officials have had
little expertise in financial management and could not benefit from the past
experience in projecting revenues and expenditures. The institutional
environment within local governments has been in the state of flux as various
organizations have been dismantled and reorganized. Because the legal
framework of local finance was enacted just before the beginning of the 1991
fiscal year, there was little time available to develop financial plans. All
these factors were bound to affect the quality of financial planning of local
governments. An overall good performance, as shown by budgets execution in
January to June 1991, has demonstrated a high degree of fiscal responsibility
of local governments.

2.   Although the period covered by financial reports is too short to make
generalizations concerning advantages and disadvantages of the current system,
it is, nonetheless, worthwhile to examine budgets executed in Jan. - June
1991. The size of a sample of local governments for which information is
available is adequate to identify emerging patterns in intergovernment fiscal
transfers, own-revenue sources and expenditures. Local governments are in a
good financial shape in stark contrast to central government budget. Contrary
to official concerns, that served to justify the imposition of caps on maximum
local tax rates and of other measures limiting fiscal autonomy of local
governments, officials responsible for gminas' finances have been extremely
prudent in financial management.

3.   The analysis of the sample of gminas based on their financial reports
submitted to the Ministry of Finance leads to one general observation
concerning relationships among various categories of expenditures and
revenues; no single significant relationship among variables identified in the
financial report format could be established. The absence of clear patterns
is surprising in some cases. For instance, although the officially declared
objective of block grants is to equalize incomes across gminas, the approved
transfers per capita bear no relationship to own-source incomes per capita.
To some extent, this absence of patterns is the result of a privileged fiscal
position of town gminas. Town budgets recorded the highest revenues per
capita in all major categories, i.e., fiscal transfers including block grants,
shared national taxes, and own-source revenues. Thus the size and allocation
of block grants by the Ministry of Finance is driven by other than income-
equalization considerations.[1] In all, tests of various hypotheses for
samples excluding town or city gminas have not yielded any significant

---

[1] The size of block grants is determined on the basis of a formula which
takes into account a whole group of factors (see Annex I). The underlying
assumption is that own-source revenues per capita are not the most important
evidence of a potentially, more difficult than the average, situation facing a
gmina. Yet this does not explain why town gminas would score higher on "non own-
source revenue" criteria.

results. This result suggests that (i) there exists considerable variation in
financial management not only between but also within classes of gminas, and
that (ii) central allotment of fiscal transfers does not take directly into
account revenue-generating capacities of local governments.

A. Sample of Local Governments: Selection Procedure and Its Economic Significance

4.   Our analysis is limited to a sample of 54 local governments selected by
the Central Office of Planning.[2] While this sample seems small when set
against the total of 2,419 local governments, it is quite substantive in terms
of population and of the coverage of city and town local governments. The
sample covers gminas inhabited by 3,173.5 thousand people, which account for
8.4 percent of the total population of Poland. The population coverage of
city and town gminas is even more extensive; the sample's urban population
accounts for 13 percent of the total population of Polish cities and towns.
The sample was not selected at random, however. The procedure is biased in
favor of urban local governments and focuses on macroregions identified for
the purpose of regional planning by the Central Office of Planning. The
extent to which gminas represent the average conditions of each macroregion is
impossible to establish, however.

5.   The analysis is limited by the format of financial reports imposed by
the Ministry of Finance. Information required by the Ministry of Finance is
general especially as it relates to own-source revenues and expenditures. The
report form contains the following categories: (1) total revenues out of which
property taxes, fees and taxes from farms and taxes on specialized
agricultural production, shared national taxes (of which: 5% of income taxes;
30% of wage taxes; 30% of honoraria taxes; 30% of income equalization taxes;
and 50% of lump sum taxes), other revenues, grant earmarked for gminas' own
functions, a grant earmarked for delegated functions, and a block grant are
specified as separate entries; (2) total expenditures out of which personnel
expenditures (of which payroll expenditures), investment expenditures, and
other expenditures are identified; (3) current account balance; (4) sources of
financing deficit of which: bank credit; surplus from previous years; and
other are identified. The report format does not cover all important
categories of expenditures and revenues. The category "other" is too large on
both revenue and expenditure side: it accounts for about one third of an
average local budget In consequence, the level of disaggregation does not
allow for a detailed analysis of either the revenue or expenditure side.

6.   The sample of gminas under examination contains 6 gminas from each of 9
macroregions of Poland.[3] Gminas have been divided into three classes: city,

---

    [2] See _Kondycja budzetow wojewodow i budzetow samorzadowych po I polroczu
1991_ (The state of voivods' and local governments' budgets after the first 6
months of 1991), Department of Social Development, Central Office of Planning,
Warsaw, September 1991.

    [3] For the purpose of regional planning, Poland is divided into nine
macroregions.

town and village. From each macroregion, two gminas belonging to every class have been selected. Each class has 18 localities, and it has distinct features. The city gminas have significantly larger average populations (151,000 as compared with 18,000 for town and 7,200 for village gminas) and very low proportion of labor employed in agriculture (3.7 percent as compared with 17.2 percent and 48.4 percent).

7.   Because of the selection procedure, the sample is biased in favor of city and to a lesser extent of town gminas. The coverage for city gminas is especially comprehensive: 18 city gminas of the sample account for 15.4 percent of all city municipalities. It contains 11 voivodship capitals of the total of 49. The scope covered by the sample is much lower for town gminas (2.6 percent) and village gminas (1.1 percent). For these reasons, generalizations and insights derived from the analysis of each class provide a better fit to the real world than the one based on averages for the total sample. By far, the most representative and comprehensive is the sample of city localities.

8.   Given the "over-representation" of urban areas, it is not surprising that the shares of the sample measured along various fiscal and economic dimensions for all local governments of the sample are substantially higher than indicated by their share in terms of the number of local governments nationwide (2.2 percent). The following list provides data describing the economic significance of the sample: **(a)** total local revenues of the sample planned for 1991 account for 11.6 percent of aggregate gmina revenues in 1991; **(b)** own source revenues of the sample approved for 1991 account for 14.6 percent of aggregate local own-source revenues (own-source revenues executed in Jan. - June 1991 by 54 local governments amounted to 12.1 percent of the total); **(c)** planned shared national taxes account for 10.5 percent of the total (shared national taxes executed amounted to 13.9 percent); **(d)** fiscal transfers to gminas of the sample account for 9.5 percent of the total transfers from central to local government approved for 1991 (the executed were slightly lower and accounted for 9.4 percent); **(e)** property taxes of the sample account for 10 percent of the total property taxes projected for 1991 (the portion actually executed in the first 6 months was 9.9 percent); **(f)** agricultural taxes of the sample account for 1.4 percent of aggregate local agriculture tax (the portion actually executed of 2.8 percent was twice as high). In all, economic significance of the sample by far outweighs its modest share in the total number of local governments in Poland.

B. Budget Execution and Emerging Patterns in Local Finance

9.   The data on the budget execution for the sample suggests that local government have adopted a very conservative approach to financial management (see Table 1). Revenues tended to be underestimated and actual expenditures turned out to be substantially lower than planned. Revenue execution was on average about 3 percent higher than planned while expenditure were 9 percent below the levels approved in local budgets for 1991. There was, however, significant variation resulting in part from errors in predicting financial inflows and in part from higher inflation than assumed by the Ministry of

Finance.[4] All local governments of the sample (except for one) registered very substantial current account surpluses. Surpluses for each group of gminas in the first 6 months of 1991 exceeded the surpluses planned for the whole year by 61 percent on average. Thus, surpluses accumulated by the mid-year have provided gminas with significant financial reserves.

Table 1.   Budget executed in Jan.-June 1991; averages for each class of gmina (in Zl. billion)

Class	Revenues		Exec.	Expenditures		Exec.	Balance		Exec.
	plan.	exec.	%	plan.	exec.	%	plan.	exec.	%
1. City gminas	255	136	53	229	95	41	26	41	159
2. Town gminas	37	18	49	33	12	36	3	6	163
3. Village gminas	8	4	55	6	2	37	2	2	130
Memo: (a) averages for the sample;	100	53	53	90	36	41	10	17	161
(b) aggregate data	5395	2856	53	4837	1959	41	557	898	161

Note: ratios of budget execution may differ because of rounding.

Source: Own calculations from data in gminas' financial reports

10.   The mission of December 1991 ascertained that the primary explanations for the high mid-year surpluses are (a) significantly higher expenditures had been committed, but not reported on a cash basis, and (b) local governmente officials in general were very cautious on the expenditure side because they were unsure if national shared and transferred revenues of the second semester would keep pace with those of the first. At year's end financing by the central government did fall off, and local budgets appear to have been reasonably balanced.

11.   Lower levels of expenditure execution in town and village gminas may be explained in part by differences in management efficiency of local governments. Village and small town gminas often have personnel with weak professional and technical skills. Underestimation of flow of revenues of city and village local governments, combined with lower than approved levels of spending, was quite significant. Lower levels of total expenditures executed by mid-year were mainly caused by a limited level of investment activities especially in town gminas. One possible explanation is the lack of institutional skills to develop and carry out capital projects, since smaller

---

[4] The extreme case is that of Warsaw Downtown (Warszawa-Srodmiescie) whose revenues executed in Jan. - June 1991 stood at 92 percent of the revenue approved for the whole year.

gminas, i.e., towns and villages, lack necessary skills and some relevant services are not easily accessible. The great variation of investment expenditures as compared with current expenditures reinforces the pertinence of this observation.

12.   Expenditures: Although the information contained in financial reports to the Ministry of Finance does not allow for a detailed analysis of local governments' expenditures,[5] the following general conclusions can be drawn from their examination. First, the execution of current expenditures reveals small variation across the whole sample (the coefficient of variation was between .19 and .23), and was below the planned level. Only 3 out of 54 gminas registered the execution ratio of current expenditures above 50 percent.[6] The execution ratio for both town and village gminas was 7 percentage points below the level of city gminas. Second, investment expenditures executed varied significantly across both classes and within each class of gminas, and execution ratios were on average higher than of current revenues. The highest variation was among town gminas, while the lowest among city gminas. Investment expenditures executed of three gminas (one in each class) were either equal or higher than planned for the whole year. In 22 gminas (6 city, 7 town, and 9 village gminas) investment execution ratios were higher than of current revenues. Local governments spent on average about 25 percent of their total revenue executed on investment. This share was smaller than planned for 1991. Third, it is noteworthy that both total and investment expenditures per capita in town gminas were significantly higher than in other classes of gminas (see Table 2). The variation in investment expenditures per capita cannot be explained in terms of population size of localities.

13.   Expenditures per capita executed in Jan. - June 1991 were significantly higher in towns than in other classes of gminas. The averages conceal a high variation within and across classes of gminas in both approved and executed investment expenditures; very significant variation of village gminas is noteworthy, since it may reflect uneven distribution of institutional capacities due to their size and available resources.

---

[5] It is restricted to capital expenditures and current expenditures desegregated into payroll and other personnel costs.

[6] The group includes one city gmina of Warszawa-Srodmiescie (Downtown Warsaw) and two town gminas--Mragowo and Nowy Tomysl. Two of these local governments had revenues execution ratios higher than fifty percent (Warsaw-Downtown of 92%, and N. Tomysl of 53%) and Mragowo of 49.5%.

Table 2:   Average expenditures per capita executed by mid-year 1991 for the sample
            of gminas (in ZL million)

Class	Current planned	Current executed	Investment planned	Investment executed	Total planned	Total executed
1. CITY GMINAS						
mean	1164	518	373	100	1532	616
standard deviation	559	352	218	62	559	359
coefficient of var.	.47	.68	.58	.61	.37	.58
2. TOWN GMINAS						
mean	1639	592	431	141	2131	760
standard deviation	553	239	367	98	651	300
coefficient of var.	.34	.40	.87	.70	.31	.40
3. VILLAGE GMINAS						
mean	660	249	225	83	834	313
standard deviation	312	116	299	96	319	128
coefficient of var.	.47	.47	1.33	1.15	.38	.41
Memorandum: total sample						
mean	1154	453	344	108	1499	563
standard deviation	629	294	313	90	749	336
coefficient of var.	.54	.65	.91	.83	.51	.63

Sources: as in Table 1

14.   Revenues: As for revenues, total local revenue execution was on average
slightly higher than planned (see Tables 2 and 3). The variation among
classes of gminas was relatively limited: it ranged between 0.55 (village) and
0.49 (city). The execution of fiscal transfers was responsible for a lower
ratio for city gminas' revenues: the execution of other major sources of city
revenues exceeded 50 percent. Leaving aside fiscal transfers to village
gminas whose execution at the level of 71 percent was probably the result of
lack of information among local village officials about earmarked and block
grants planned by the government for 1991, there were several factors
responsible for the inflow of revenues exceeding expectations. First, local
budgets were less affected by the recession than central budgets, because
shared national taxes turned out to be less sensitive to the deteriorating
macroeconomic situation in 1991. Inflationary increases in wages and other
personal incomes were accountable for shared tax revenues higher than planned
which offset the drop in enterprise income taxes. Wage, payroll and honoraria
taxes executed exceeded significantly the planned levels. Second, local
revenues benefitted from the expansion of the private sector. Lump sum taxes
levied on small businesses were 60 percent higher in Jan. - June 1991 than
planned for the whole year. Third, own-source revenues executed also exceeded
expectations especially for village gminas. Although property and agriculture
taxes are often paid in lump sums at the beginning of a year, and one would

Table 3:   Revenue execution in Jan. - June 1991 by source and shares in
            average total local revenues for a sample of gminas

Source	Ratio of execution				Share in average local revenue executed (in %)			
	(a)	(b)	(c)	(d)	(a)	(b)	(c)	(d)
A. Fiscal Transfers	.56	.47	.71	.49	21.2	19.8	20.8	29.2
A.1. own functions	.64	.42	.34	.94	1.0	0.3	0.3	2.2
A.2. delegated functions	.49	.46	.44	.38	8.9	9.3	11.6	7.9
A.3. block grant	.50	.49	.48	.53	11.3	10.5	8.9	19.1
B. Shared National Taxes	.59	.50	.54	.72	31.2	31.5	31.8	18.7
B.1. corporate income	.30	.30	.21	.39	5.9	5.9	6.5	2.1
B.2. payroll	.75	.54	.56	1.14	17.1	17.6	15.9	6.9
B.3. honoraria	1.03	.86	.92	1.29	2.9	3.0	2.4	2.2
B.4. income equalization	1.33	1.28	1.47	1.25	1.0	1.0	.8	.6
B.5. lump sum	1.62	1.35	1.05	2.45	4.3	4.0	6.2	6.9
C. Own-Source Revenues	.61	.56	.59	.66	49.1	48.8	49.7	54.3
C.1. property tax	.59	.63	.53	.62	14.0	13.4	18.9	13.3
C.2. agriculture tax	.63	.59	.78	.52	.8	.1	3.3	8.1
C.3. other local revenues	.74	.57	.64	1.00	34.3	35.3	27.7	32.9
Memo: total local revenue execution	.53	.49	.53	.55				

Notes: The figures do not necessarily add up to 100, because of rounding.
            (a) - averages for the whole sample; (b)--city gminas; (c)--town
            gminas; (d)--village gminas

Source: as in Table 1

expect, therefore, a higher level of execution, other own-source revenues were
accountable for a good financial performance.[7] Finally, the average share of
own-source revenues executed for city and village gminas was higher than
planned: for the whole sample, the share executed in the mid-year was 49.1
percent as compared with 43.4 percent planned for 1991; for city gminas, 48.8
and 42.2 percent; for town gminas, 50 and 51.1 percent; and, for village
gminas, 54.4 and 48.5 percent. The shares of both fiscal transfers and shared
national taxes were lower than planned except for fiscal transfers to town
gminas (20.8% as compared with planned 17%).

15.   The fall in shares actually executed as compared with local budgets
approved for 1991 stemmed not from their unexpected contraction but
"unplanned" buoyancy of other sources of national shared revenues. As can be
seen from Tables 3 and 4, the contributions of shared national revenue-raising
instruments approved for 1991 significantly differed from actually executed in
Jan. - June 1991. The fall in incomes of state-owned enterprises and the

---

    [7] Unfortunately, they are not desegregated in financial reports of local
governments, although they account on average for more than 30 percent of total
revenues.

increase of private activities was a major factor shaping financial situation
of local governments. As a result, tax revenues from private sector
activities substantially expanded whereas from state-owned enterprises
contracted significantly. The largest change was in revenues from "individual
business" lump sum tax in which local governments have a larger share (50
percent) than in other national shared taxes.[8] As can be seen from Table 4,
its share in national revenues in creased from 15 to 27 percent, or by 80
percent. This increase was closely followed by taxes levied on professional
fees and honoraria. Revenues from personal income-equalization tax imposed on
the wealthiest segment of the population also increased, although its share in
shared national tax revenues has remained small. The authorities, setting up
the ground for the introduction of PIT in 1992, did not change the threshold
above which incomes are subject to extra taxation. As a result, with
inflation running in 1991 at around 40 percent, the base of this tax
significantly has increased.

Table 4:   The planned and executed composition of shared national
           tax revenues in 1991 (in percent)

Revenue-raising instrument	Planned	Executed (by June 1991)	Percent change in shared
Corporate Income Tax	25.1	13.2	(-)47.4
Payroll Tax	53.6	33.2	(-)38.1
Honoraria Tax	8.7	14.1	(+)62.1
Income-Equalization Tax	3.1	4.3	(+)38.7
Lump Sum Tax	15.1	27.3	(+)80.8

Source: as in Table 1

16.   Table 5 summarizes local revenues per capita for each class of local
governments of the sample. They again point to a "privileged" position of
town gminas. Their average revenues per capita is 89 percent higher than of
village gminas and 21 percent than of city gminas. They outperformed on a per
capita basis other classes of gminas in all major categories of revenues.
While lower own source revenues per capita of village gminas were compensated
for by larger block grants, this was not the case for city gminas. Although
they had lower own source revenues and from shared national taxes, city gminas
had the lowest block grants per capita. It is not clear why the composition
of revenues of city governments differs so substantially from that of towns.
Corporate income taxes and property taxes, both executed and approved for
1991, accounted for a larger share of towns than of other gmina-classes.
Without more disagregated data currently lumped in "other" expenditures or
revenues, not much can be inferred why town gminas turned to have more
resources on a per capita basis than others.

_____

    [8] For the explanation of a lump sum or individual business tax, see Annex
I, para. 6.

Table 5:   Average planned and executed revenues per capita of each type of gminas

Type of gminas	Total Fiscal Transfers		Block Grant		Shared National Taxes		Own-source Revenues		Total Revenues	
	Planned (in ZL million)	Executed	Planned (in ZL million)	Executed	Planned (in ZL million)	Executed	Planned (in ZL million)	Executed	Planned (in ZL million)	Executed
1. CITY GMINAS										
group mean	385.93	160.29	173.94	78.72	515.39	246.99	694.03	395.77	1595.35	803.05
std. deviation	382.26	139.43	172.70	76.01	93.84	51.99	556.76	512.46	571.49	543.28
coef. variation	0.85	0.87	0.99	0.97	0.18	0.21	0.80	1.29	0.36	0.68
2. TOWN GMINAS										
group mean	457.45	240.24	272.05	131.11	565.49	269.55	950.57	523.25	1973.52	1033.04
std. deviation	303.99	141.43	222.97	111.84	373.22	195.48	447.27	264.58	708.81	439.51
coef. variation	0.66	0.59	0.82	0.85	0.66	0.73	0.47	0.51	0.36	0.43
3. VILLAGE GMINAS										
group mean	432.50	194.64	256.09	123.91	162.90	92.97	515.37	321.41	1073.40	593.79
std. deviation	359.12	150.81	148.23	77.57	324.53	163.64	425.29	275.37	863.04	467.77
coef. variation	0.83	0.77	0.58	0.63	1.99	1.76	0.83	0.86	0.80	0.79

C. Intergovernment Fiscal Transfers

17.   Gminas receive three types of grants: two are earmarked for
administrative functions performed by local governments (own and delegated)
and a block grant. Since gminas in the sample absorbed (and are scheduled to
obtain) about 9.5 percent of total fiscal transfers in 1991), conclusions from
the data for the sample can be generalized for all gminas.[9] The execution of
fiscal transfers was effected according to the schedule (this was also
confirmed by local official interviewed during the mission's field trip. The
composition and distribution of transfers raises substantial concerns related
to their low transparency, limited controls on spending, and possible impact
of delegated functions not accompanied by the delegation of authority on the
operation of local governments. In brief, the current system of earmarked
transfers does not provide incentives and flexibility to enhance expenditure
management and service delivery, and block grants bear no relationship to own-
source revenues per capita of gminas. A caveat should be made, however.
Since the financial report format does not distinguish between transfers
related to four criteria used by the Ministry of Finance to determine a total
fiscal transfer to a local government (see Annex 1, p. 4 and 5), the
conclusions are tentative until a further, closer, examination. It is
indicative of poor monitoring and accounting practice, however, that major
components as they relate to official criteria have not been identified in a
financial report format prepared by the Ministry of Finance.

18.   **Transfers earmarked for delegated functions**: Earmarked transfers fall
into two groups: the first are designated to cover the provision of
administrative services assigned to local governments by law (own functions),

---

[9] Earmarked transfers of the sample account for 10.4 percent of aggregate
earmarked transfers approved (and 9.6 percent executed. The shares of the sample
in aggregate block grants are 8.8 percent (approved) and 9.2 percent (executed).

and the second by a contract with a voivodship office (delegated functions). Each raises different kind of problems: the latter blurs the distinction between state administration and representative local government, and the former unnecessarily introduces room for bargaining between central and local government. As far as delegated functions are concerned, their impact on local government is significant: they account on average for almost one tenth of total local revenues. Local governments' involvement--quite notable in terms of funds transferred from central government and which reportedly is to be expanded--in performing functions on behalf of voivodship offices may turn out to be damaging politically. Local governments risk become identified in public perception with the central government administration. As a result, they will take blame for activities over which they have very limited authority. There are other more palpable dangers. The distribution of earmarked transfers is not formula driven, and is subject to administrative haggling. Although local governments have discretion in the choice of delegated functions, once they make a decision, some portion of their activities consists in acting on behalf of the central administration. It introduces an extra link of subordination to central authorities which defies the idea of autonomy inherent in the Local Self-Government Act. Another problem is that in the absence of good accounting information, there is a potential for bargaining and conflicts within the general government.

19.   Transfers earmarked for local government own functions: As for transfers subsidizing own functions of local governments, the rules governing their apportionment and size are obscure. It is unclear why some local budgets have been subsidized and others have not. The largest number of recipients was among city gminas (4), followed by town (3) and village gminas (3). One city (Zamosc) and one town gmina (Starogard) had a transfer approved in its budget but not executed by June 30, 1991. The reverse situation occurred for one city; Lublin received a transfer earmarked for its own functions, although it was not planned. While the average share of transfers earmarked for own functions in total fiscal transfers executed was low, it was significant for its recipients: for village recipients, they ranged between 30 and 37 percent; for towns, shares were 14 and 37 percent; and, for cities, they were between 7 and 20 percent. Transfers were not negatively correlated to either low own-source or total local revenues per capita. Using these criteria, a different set of gminas would be eligible for subsidies.

20.   Block grants: The most important component--quite understandably, given its objective of welfare equalization across gminas-- of fiscal transfers, both planned and executed, was block grant: its average share was about 50 percent of total transfers from central to local governments of the sample with village gminas recording the highest share (see Table 5). The use of various statistical methods to identify factors explaining the variation in block grants per capita did not yield any significant results.[10] Similarly,

---

[10]   Neither correlation matrix including revenues and expenditures per capita nor stepwise regression and tests for interaction among variables produced viable candidates. Analyses were conducted separately for all gminas, and for each class.

coefficients of variation for each class of gminas were not markedly different for total revenues per capita including and excluding block grants.[11]

21.   Details of the sample gmina budgets are provided in the following Tables 6-7.

---

[11] The exclusion of a planned block grant per capita from planned total revenues per capita increased the coefficient from .36 to .40 for city gminas, from .36 to .43 for town gminas, and from .80 to .99 for village gminas. Thus except for village gminas, its impact on income equalization is negligible.

Table 6 (Page 1 of 3)

Executed Gmina Budget Data for a Sample of Gminas
Jan.-June 1991, in Zl. Billions

URBAN GMINAS	Pop. ('000)	Local Revenues (Zl.billion) Own-Source + Shared			Fiscal Transfers (Zl. billion)			Total Local Revenues (Zl. billion)			Per Capita Planned Revenues (1991 -Zl. '000)			Expenditures Total			Current			% employed in agr./forest.
		Planned (a)	Executed (b)	Ratio (b)/(a)	Planned (a)	Executed (b)	Ratio (b)/(a)	Planned (a)	Executed (b)	Ratio (b)/(a)	Loc Rev	Transfers	Total	Planned (a)	Executed (b)	Ratio (b)/(a)	Planned (a)	Executed (b)	Ratio (b)/(a)	
1. Bialystok	268.1	266.0	132.2	0.46	18.0	9.0	0.50	304.0	141.2	0.46	1067	67	1134	286	124.7	0.44	233.5	101.7	0.44	4.10
2. Olsztyn	161.2	357.7	131.7	0.37	72.6	36.3	0.50	430.3	168.0	0.39	2219	450	2669	357.7	131	0.37	300.2	118.4	0.39	4.10
3. Zabrze	203.4	286.7	182.7	0.64	59.2	29.6	0.50	345.9	212.3	0.61	1410	291	1701	286.7	96	0.33	232.3	84	0.36	1.20
4. Bytom	229.9	391.7	208.3	0.53	48.6	24.7	0.51	440.3	233.0	0.53	1706	211	1915	391.7	129.3	0.33	281.6	114.9	0.41	1.20
5. Nowa Sred	157.6	504.5	461.9	0.92	1.6	0.8	0.50	506.1	462.7	0.91	3201	10	3211	504.5	315.5	0.63	442.3	293.3	0.61	0.90
6. Radom	226.3	335.2	190.7	0.57	111.4	55.7	0.50	446.6	246.4	0.55	1481	492	1973	335.2	144	0.43	283.6	124.4	0.44	3.80
7. Lublin	80.8	95.5	64.9	0.68	9.6	4.8	0.50	105.1	69.7	0.66	1182	119	1301	95.5	53.9	0.56	73	50.7	0.69	3.20
8. Nowa Sol	43.1	54	21.8	0.40	2.8	1.5	0.54	56.8	23.3	0.41	1253	65	1318	54	16.1	0.30	40.9	13.6	0.33	3.60
9. Lublin	349.7	396.3	215.9	0.54	23.4	11.7	0.50	419.7	227.6	0.54	1133	67	1200	396.3	193.3	0.49	253.9	104.3	0.41	4.10
10. Zamosc	60.7	143.5	37.6	0.26	7.1	3.5	0.49	150.6	41.1	0.27	2364	117	2481	143.5	36	0.25	76.3	29.9	0.39	6.90
11. Kielce	212.9	255.7	116.1	0.45	15.1	7.5	0.50	270.8	123.6	0.46	1201	71	1272	255.7	88.5	0.35	174.6	74	0.42	4.00
12. Rzeszow	150.7	267.8	113.8	0.42	10.1	5.1	0.50	277.9	118.9	0.43	1777	67	1844	267.8	75.3	0.28	182.4	68.8	0.38	4.70
13. Konin	79.7	93.5	47.2	0.50	5.6	2.8	0.50	99.1	50.0	0.50	1173	70	1243	93.5	36.3	0.39	70.3	28.3	0.40	4.80
14. Kalisz	106.1	131.2	54.3	0.41	7.1	3.6	0.51	138.3	57.9	0.42	1237	67	1303	131.2	42.3	0.32	88.4	36.3	0.41	4.30
15. Koszalin	107.6	165.1	69.2	0.42	7.2	3.6	0.50	172.3	72.8	0.42	1534	67	1601	165.1	67	0.41	100.8	39.5	0.39	3.60
16. Elblag	125.1	212	100.5	0.47	56.7	28.8	0.51	268.7	129.3	0.48	1695	453	2148	212	95.2	0.45	197.2	84.6	0.44	3.70
17. Piotr.Tryb	80.6	74.1	32.1	0.43	5.3	2.6	0.49	79.4	34.7	0.44	919	66	985	72.3	28.5	0.39	47.3	20.3	0.43	5.50
18. Pabianice	74.8	78.1	37.9	0.49	5.2	2.6	0.50	83.3	40.5	0.49	1044	70	1114	78.1	33.8	0.43	64.2	25.5	0.40	2.90
GROUP MEAN	151.0	229.4	123.3	0.54	25.9	13.0	0.50	255.3	136.3	0.53	1519	172	1690.47	229.27	94.83	0.40	176.82	78.58	0.43	3.70
STD. DEVIATION	80.61	129.49	102.60	0.14	30.01	15.06	0.01	145.55	107.25	0.11	557.70	151.23	599.22	129.61	71.11	0.09	114.83	63.22	0.08	1.45
COEF. VARIATION	0.53	0.56	0.83	0.26	1.16	1.16	0.02	0.57	0.79	0.25	0.37	0.88	0.35	0.57	0.75	0.24	0.65	0.80	0.19	0.39

Table 6 (Page 2 of 3)

Executed Gmina Budget Data for a Sample of Gminas
Jan.-June 1991, in Zł. billions

TOWN GMINAS	Pop. ('000)	Local Revenues (Zł.billion) Own-Source + Shared			Fiscal Transfers (Zł. billion)			Total Local Revenues (Zł. billion)			Per Capita Planned Revenues (1991 -Zł.'000)			Expenditures Total			Current			% employed in agr./forest.
		Planned (a)	Executed (b)	Ratio (b)/(a)	Planned (a)	Executed (b)	Ratio (b)/(a)	Planned (a)	Executed (b)	Ratio (b)/(a)	Loc Rev	Transfers	Total	Planned (a)	Executed (b)	Ratio (b)/(a)	Planned (a)	Executed (b)	Ratio (b)/(a)	
1. Mragowo	21.8	29.5	14.6	0.49	9.3	4.7	0.49	39.0	19.3	0.49	1353	436	1789	29.5	13	0.44	24.3	13	0.53	54.80
2. Grojec	6.4	21.9	11.2	0.51	1.4	0.7	0.50	23.3	11.9	0.51	3318	212	3530	21.9	8.7	0.40	13.9	5.4	0.39	7.10
3. Brzeszcze	12.7	38	19.8	0.52	6.4	3.2	0.50	44.4	23.0	0.52	2992	504	3496	38	9.8	0.26	20	6	0.30	18.50
4. Skawier	5.5	15.4	7.3	0.47	0.9	0.4	0.44	16.3	7.7	0.47	2808	164	2964	15.4	3.5	0.23	13.3	3	0.23	34.20
5. Piaseczno	24.3	57	30.3	0.53	1.1	0.2	0.14	58.4	30.5	0.52	2344	58	2403	57	31.8	0.56	52.7	24.9	0.47	5.00
6. Szydłowiec	12.1	20.4	6	0.29	4.6	1.3	0.28	25.0	7.3	0.27	1686	380	2066	20.4		0.34	19.9	6.7	0.34	12.20
7. Lomna	4.7	12.4	4.9	0.40	2.7	1.3	0.48	15.1	6.2	0.41	2638	374	3013	12.4	4.7	0.38	11.4	3.4	0.32	9.70
8. Milicz	12.1	21.1	15.1	0.72	3.2	1.6	0.50	24.3	16.7	0.69	1774	264	2008	21.1	8	0.38	20.6	7.8	0.38	16.60
9. Terspol	5.8	11.2	7	0.63	3.2	2.3	0.58	15.8	9.3	0.59	1931	793	2726	11.2	2.0	0.26	9.5	2.4	0.27	8.80
10. Lubin	6.9	12.8	4.9	0.38	0.8	0.4	0.50	13.6	5.3	0.39	1855	116	1971	12.8	4.4	0.34	8	2.9	0.36	18.80
11. Janio	37.1	60.4	33.1	0.55	2.1	1	0.48	62.5	34.1	0.55	1628	57	1685	60.4	21.4	0.35	36.6	11.8	0.32	11.50
12. Polanice	7.4	21.8	11.5	0.53	4.6	2.3	0.50	26.4	13.6	0.52	2944	622	3566	21.8	5.7	0.26	14.8	4.3	0.29	8.10
13. K. Trzepi	8.2	20.5	14.4	0.80	1.2	0.9	0.75	21.7	17.3	0.80	2500	146	2646	20.5	11.5	0.56	14.2	9.6	0.53	7.70
14. Golanci	3.4	8	4.2	0.53	1.2	0.6	0.50	9.2	4.8	0.52	2353	353	2706	8	3.2	0.40	7	2.7	0.39	33.00
15. Solmujscie	42.9	108	31.2	0.29	3.4	2.2	0.65	111.4	33.4	0.30	2517	79	2597	108	26.9	0.25	80.9	23.7	0.29	1.70
16. Starowardzu	49.2	54.6	29.7	0.54	3.2	1.6	0.50	57.8	31.3	0.54	1110	65	1175	54.6	20.3	0.37	44.5	18	0.40	49.00
17. Skierniewice	44.2	66	37	0.56	2.8	1.3	0.46	68.8	38.3	0.56	1493	63	1557	66	19.3	0.29	31.6	11	0.35	6.80
18. Losk	19.5	22.4	10.8	0.48	3.6	1.8	0.50	26.0	12.6	0.48	1149	185	1333	22.4	9.7	0.43	15.1	6.4	0.42	5.70
GROUP MEAN	18.0	33.4	16.4	0.49	3.2	1.3	0.50	36.6	17.9	0.49	1856	178	2031.00	33.41	11.77	0.36	26.57	9.06	0.37	17.18
STD. DEVIATION	14.82	25.39	10.76	0.12	2.15	1.09	0.12	25.58	10.87	0.12	651.39	218.77	737.69	25.39	8.40	0.09	18.36	4.7	0.08	15.01
COEF. VARIATION	0.82	0.76	0.66	0.25	0.67	0.70	0.24	0.70	0.61	0.24	0.35	1.23	0.36	0.76	0.71	0.26	0.75	0.7	0.22	0.87

Table 6 (Page 3 of 3)

Executed Gmina Budget Data for a Sample of Gmines
Jan.-June 1991, in Zl. Billions

VILLAGE GMINAS	Pop. ('000)	Local Revenues (Zl.billion) Own-Source + Shared			Fiscal Transfers (Zl. billion)			Total Local Revenues (Zl. billion)			Per Capita Planned Revenues (1991 -Zl. '000)			Expenditures Total			Expenditures Current			% employed in agr./forest.
		Planned (a)	Executed (b)	Ratio (b)/(a)	Planned (a)	Executed (b)	Ratio (b)/(a)	Planned (a)	Executed (b)	Ratio (b)/(a)	Loc Rev	Transfers	Total	Planned (a)	Executed (b)	Ratio (b)/(a)	Planned (a)	Executed (b)	Ratio (b)/(a)	
1. Prostki	7.7	5	2.6	0.52	1.1	0.6	0.55	6.1	3.2	0.52	649	143	792	5	2	0.40	4.8	1.8	0.38	51.10
2. Krynki	4.1	3.4	1.4	0.41	0.7	0.1	0.14	4.1	1.5	0.37	829	171	1000	3.4	1.4	0.41	3.4	1.4	0.41	50.50
3. Lubomia	7.9	7	4	0.57	3.5	1.7	0.49	10.5	5.7	0.54	886	443	1329	7	3.1	0.44	5.2	2.2	0.42	19.70
4. Babice	8	9	6	0.67	3.3	1.7	0.52	12.3	7.7	0.63	1125	413	1538	9	3.4	0.38	4.6	1.4	0.30	30.80
5. Maltinia Gorna	12.7	7.7	4.3	0.56	1	0.8	0.80	8.7	5.1	0.59	606	79	685	7.7	3.9	0.51	5	3.1	0.62	30.10
6. Dobra	6.3	6.9	6	0.87	1.4	0.7	0.50	8.3	6.7	0.81	1095	222	1317	6.9	1.9	0.28	4.6	1.3	0.28	57.60
7. Boleslawiec	10.2	11.5	9.3	0.81	0.9	0.6	0.67	12.4	9.9	0.80	1127	88	1216	11.5	3.6	0.31	11	3.5	0.32	42.30
8. Vinsko	9.2	4.4	2.7	0.42	1.8	0.7	0.39	8.2	3.4	0.41	696	196	891	6.4	1.9	0.30	4.5	1.2	0.27	49.10
9. Wertkowice	11.5	9.1	5.8	0.64	0.8	0.4	0.50	9.9	6.2	0.63	791	70	861	9.1	4	0.44	7.1	2.7	0.38	55.90
10. Siedliszcze	7.9	6.6	2.4	0.34	2.6	1.2	0.44	9.2	3.6	0.39	835	329	1165	6.6	1.8	0.27	6.6	0.9	0.30	56.10
11. Bircza	6.8	5.2	2.8	0.54	3	1	0.33	8.2	3.8	0.46	765	441	1206	5.2	2.2	0.42	4.8	1.9	0.40	62.60
12. Manice	8	6.4	4	0.63	2.4	1.2	0.50	8.8	5.2	0.59	800	300	1100	6.4	2.3	0.36	5.2	1.9	0.37	33.00
13. Tulicz	6.1	3.8	3.3	0.87	1.4	0.7	0.50	5.2	4	0.77	623	230	852	3.8	1.8	0.47	3.8	1.8	0.47	56.10
14. Koscielec	6.6	5.9	2.8	0.47	2.9	1.4	0.48	8.8	4.2	0.48	894	439	1333	5.9	1.9	0.32	5.4	1.9	0.35	44.00
15. Cedry Wielkie	5.5	6.5	5.1	0.76	2	1	0.50	8.5	6.1	0.72	1182	364	1545	6.5	2.2	0.34	4.6	2.1	0.46	48.60
16. Letkowo	3.4	2.9	0.7	0.24	0.2	0.1	0.50	3.1	0.8	0.26	853	59	912	2.9	0.9	0.31	2.1	0.7	0.33	66.40
17. Brojce	5	3.4	1.9	0.56	1.3	0.7	0.54	4.7	2.6	0.55	680	260	940	3.4	1.6	0.47	2.5	1	0.40	52.90
18. Wadkierody	3.2	2.2	0.9	0.41	0.6	0.3	0.50	2.8	1.2	0.43	688	187	875	2.2	0.6	0.27	2.2	0.6	0.27	64.50
GROUP MEAN	7.2	6.1	3.7	0.61	1.7	0.8	0.50	7.8	4.5	0.58	837	238	1074.51	6.05	2.25	0.37	4.66	1.74	0.37	48.41
STD. DEVIATION	2.52	2.34	2.11	0.17	0.98	0.46	0.13	2.78	2.28	0.15	177.73	130.82	249.44	2.34	0.95	0.07	1.97	0.77	0.08	12.56
COEF. VARIATION	0.35	0.39	0.57	0.28	0.57	0.56	0.25	0.36	0.51	0.26	0.21	0.55	0.23	0.39	0.42	0.20	0.42	0.44	0.26	0.26

Table 7 (Page 1 of 3)

Executed Gmina Budget Data for a Sample of Gminas
Jan.-June 1991, in Zl. Billions

urban gminas	Local Revenues (Zl.billion) Own-Source + Shared			Fiscal Transfers (Zl. billion)			Total Local Revenues (Zl. billion)			Total Expenditures			Current Account Balance	
	Planned (a)	Executed (b)	Ratio (b)/(a)	Planned (a)	Executed (b)	Ratio (b)/(a)	Planned (a)	Executed (b)	Ratio (b)/(a)	Planned (a)	Executed (b)	Ratio (b)/(a)	Planned	Executed
1. Bialystok	286.0	132.2	0.46	18.0	9.0	0.50	304.0	141.2	0.46	286.00	124.70	0.44	18.00	16.50
2. Olsztyn	357.70	131.7	0.37	72.6	36.3	0.50	430.3	168.0	0.39	357.70	131.00	0.37	72.60	37.00
3. Zabrze	286.70	182.70	0.64	59.20	29.60	0.50	345.9	212.3	0.61	286.70	96.00	0.33	59.20	116.30
4. Bytom	391.70	208.30	0.53	48.60	24.70	0.51	440.3	233.0	0.53	391.70	129.30	0.33	48.60	103.70
5. W-wa Srod	504.50	461.90	0.92	1.60	0.80	0.50	506.1	462.7	0.91	504.50	315.50	0.63	1.60	147.20
6. Radom	335.20	190.70	0.57	111.40	55.70	0.50	446.6	246.4	0.55	335.20	144.00	0.43	111.40	102.40
7. Lubin	95.50	64.90	0.68	9.60	4.80	0.50	105.1	69.7	0.66	95.50	53.90	0.56	9.60	15.80
8. Nowa Sol	54.00	21.80	0.40	2.80	1.50	0.54	56.8	23.3	0.41	54.00	16.10	0.30	2.80	7.20
9. Lublin	396.30	215.90	0.54	23.40	11.70	0.50	419.7	227.6	0.54	396.30	193.30	0.49	23.40	34.30
10. Zamosc	143.50	37.60	0.26	7.10	3.50	0.49	150.6	41.1	0.27	143.50	36.00	0.25	7.10	5.10
11. Kielce	255.70	116.10	0.45	15.10	7.50	0.50	270.8	123.6	0.46	255.70	88.50	0.35	15.10	35.10
12. Rzeszow	267.80	113.80	0.42	10.10	5.10	0.50	277.9	118.9	0.43	267.80	75.50	0.28	10.10	43.40
13. Konin	93.50	47.20	0.50	5.60	2.80	0.50	99.1	50.0	0.50	93.50	36.30	0.39	5.60	13.70
14. Kalisz	131.20	54.30	0.41	7.10	3.60	0.51	138.3	57.9	0.42	131.20	42.30	0.32	7.10	15.60
15. Koszalin	165.10	69.20	0.42	7.20	3.60	0.50	172.3	72.8	0.42	165.10	67.00	0.41	7.20	5.80
16. Elblag	212.00	100.50	0.47	56.70	28.80	0.51	268.7	129.3	0.48	212.00	95.20	0.45	56.70	34.10
17. Piotr.Tryb	74.10	32.10	0.43	5.30	2.60	0.49	79.4	34.7	0.44	72.30	28.50	0.39	7.10	6.20
18. Pabianice	78.10	37.90	0.49	5.20	2.60	0.50	83.3	40.5	0.49	78.10	33.80	0.43	5.20	6.70
GROUP MEAN	229.4	123.3	0.54	25.9	13.0	0.50	255.3	136.3	0.50	229.27	94.83	0.40	26.02	41.45
STD. DEVIATION	129.49	102.60	0.14	30.01	15.04	0.01	145.55	107.25	0.13	129.61	71.11	0.09	29.94	43.13
COEF. VARIATION	0.56	0.83	0.26	1.16	1.16	0.02	0.57	0.79	0.26	0.57	0.75	0.24	1.15	1.04

Table 7 (Page 2 of 3)

Executed Gmina Budget Data for a Sample of Gminas
Jan.-June 1991, in Zl. Billions

TOWN GMINAS	Local Revenues (Zl.billion) Own-Source + Shared			Fiscal Transfers (Zl. billion)			Total Local Revenues (Zl. billion)			Total Expenditures			Current Account Balance	
	Planned (a)	Executed (b)	Ratio (b)/(a)	Planned (a)	Executed (b)	Ratio (b)/(a)	Planned (a)	Executed (b)	Ratio (b)/(a)	Planned (a)	Executed (b)	Ratio (b)/(a)	Planned	Executed
1. Mragowo	29.50	14.60	0.49	9.50	4.70	0.49	39.0	19.3	0.49	29.50	13.00	0.44	9.50	6.30
2. Grajewo	21.90	11.20	0.51	1.40	0.70	0.50	23.3	11.9	0.51	21.90	8.70	0.40	1.40	3.20
3. Brzeszcze	38.00	19.80	0.52	6.40	3.20	0.50	44.4	23.0	0.52	38.00	9.80	0.26	6.40	13.20
4. Siewierz	15.40	7.30	0.47	0.90	0.40	0.44	16.3	7.7	0.47	15.40	3.50	0.23	0.90	4.20
5. Piaseczno	57.00	30.30	0.53	1.40	0.20	0.14	58.4	30.5	0.52	57.00	31.80	0.56	1.40	-1.30
6. Szydlowiec	20.40	6.00	0.29	4.60	1.30	0.28	25.0	7.3	0.29	20.40	7.00	0.34	4.60	0.30
7. Lesna	12.40	4.90	0.40	2.70	1.30	0.48	15.1	6.2	0.41	12.40	4.70	0.38	2.70	1.50
8. Milicz	21.10	15.10	0.72	3.20	1.60	0.50	24.3	16.7	0.69	21.10	8.00	0.38	3.20	8.70
9. Terespol	11.20	7.00	0.63	4.60	2.30	0.50	15.8	9.3	0.59	11.20	2.90	0.26	4.60	6.40
10. Losice	12.80	4.90	0.38	0.80	0.40	0.50	13.6	5.3	0.39	12.80	4.40	0.34	0.80	0.90
11. Jaslo	60.40	33.10	0.55	2.10	1.00	0.48	62.5	34.1	0.55	60.40	21.40	0.35	2.10	12.70
12. Polaniec	21.80	11.50	0.53	4.60	2.30	0.50	26.4	13.8	0.52	21.80	5.70	0.26	4.60	8.10
13. N. Tomysl	20.50	16.40	0.80	1.20	0.90	0.75	21.7	17.3	0.80	20.50	11.50	0.56	1.20	5.80
14. Golancz	8.00	4.20	0.53	1.20	0.60	0.50	9.2	4.8	0.52	8.00	3.20	0.40	1.20	1.60
15. Swinoujscie	108.00	31.20	0.29	3.40	2.20	0.65	111.4	33.4	0.30	108.00	26.90	0.25	3.40	6.50
16. Starogard Gd.	54.60	29.70	0.54	3.20	1.60	0.50	57.8	31.3	0.54	54.60	20.30	0.37	3.20	11.00
17. Skierniewice	66.00	37.00	0.56	2.80	1.30	0.46	68.8	38.3	0.56	66.00	19.30	0.29	2.80	19.00
18. Lask	22.40	10.80	0.48	3.60	1.80	0.50	26.0	12.6	0.48	22.40	9.70	0.43	3.60	2.90
GROUP MEAN	33.4	16.4	0.5	3.2	1.5	0.5	36.6	17.9	0.5	33.4	11.8	0.36	3.20	6.17
STD. DEVIATION	25.39	10.76	0.12	2.15	1.09	0.12	25.58	10.87	0.12	25.39	8.40	0.09	2.15	5.13
COEF. VARIATION	0.76	0.66	0.24	0.67	0.70	0.25	0.70	0.61	0.23	0.76	0.71	0.26	0.67	0.83

Table 7 (Page 3 of 3)

Executed Gmina Budget Data for a Sample of Gminas
Jan.-June 1991, in Zl. Billions.

VILLAGE GMINAS	Local Revenues (Zl.billion) Own-Source + Shared			Fiscal Transfers (Zl. billion)			Total Local Revenues (Zl. billion)			Total Expenditures			Current Account Balance	
	Planned (a)	Executed (b)	Ratio (b)/(a)	Planned (a)	Executed (b)	Ratio (b)/(a)	Planned (a)	Executed (b)	Ratio (b)/(a)	Planned (a)	Executed (b)	Ratio (b)/(a)	Planned	Executed
1. Prostki	5.00	2.60	0.52	1.10	0.60	0.55	6.1	3.2	0.52	5.00	2.00	0.40	1.10	1.20
2. Krynki	3.40	1.40	0.41	0.70	0.10	0.14	4.1	1.5	0.37	3.40	1.40	0.41	0.70	0.10
3. Lubomia	7.00	4.00	0.57	3.50	1.70	0.49	10.5	5.7	0.54	7.00	3.10	0.44	3.50	2.60
4. Babice	9.00	6.00	0.67	3.30	1.70	0.52	12.3	7.7	0.63	9.00	3.40	0.38	3.30	4.30
5. Malkinia Gorna	7.70	4.30	0.56	1.00	0.80	0.80	8.7	5.1	0.59	7.70	3.90	0.51	1.00	1.20
6. Dobre	6.90	6.00	0.87	1.40	0.70	0.50	8.3	6.7	0.81	6.90	1.90	0.28	1.40	4.80
7. Boleslawiec	11.50	9.30	0.81	0.90	0.60	0.67	12.4	9.9	0.80	11.50	3.60	0.31	0.90	6.30
8. Winsko	6.40	2.70	0.42	1.80	0.70	0.39	8.2	3.4	0.41	6.40	1.90	0.30	1.80	1.50
9. Werbkowice	9.10	5.80	0.64	0.80	0.40	0.50	9.9	6.2	0.63	9.10	4.00	0.44	0.80	2.20
10. Siedliszcze	6.60	2.40	0.36	2.60	1.20	0.46	9.2	3.6	0.39	6.60	1.80	0.27	2.60	1.80
11. Bircza	5.20	2.80	0.54	3.00	1.00	0.33	8.2	3.8	0.46	5.20	2.20	0.42	3.00	1.60
12. Maslow	6.40	4.00	0.63	2.40	1.20	0.50	8.8	5.2	0.59	6.40	2.30	0.36	2.40	2.90
13. Kwilcz	3.80	3.30	0.87	1.40	0.70	0.50	5.2	4.0	0.77	3.80	1.80	0.47	1.40	2.20
14. Koscielec	5.90	2.80	0.47	2.90	1.40	0.48	8.8	4.2	0.48	5.90	1.90	0.32	2.90	2.30
15. Cedry Wielkie	6.50	5.10	0.78	2.00	1.00	0.50	8.5	6.1	0.72	6.50	2.20	0.34	2.00	3.90
16. Lelkowo	2.90	0.70	0.24	0.20	0.10	0.50	3.1	0.8	0.26	2.90	0.90	0.31	0.20	-0.10
17. Brojce	3.40	1.90	0.56	1.30	0.70	0.54	4.7	2.6	0.55	3.40	1.60	0.47	1.30	1.00
18. Wodzierady	2.20	0.90	0.41	0.60	0.30	0.50	2.8	1.2	0.43	2.20	0.60	0.27	0.60	0.60
GROUP MEAN	6.1	3.7	0.61	1.7	0.8	0.50	7.8	4.5	0.55	6.05	2.25	0.37	1.72	
STD. DEVIATION	2.34	2.11	0.17	0.98	0.46	0.13	2.78	2.28	0.15	2.34	0.95	0.07	0.44	
COEF. VARIATION	0.39	0.57	0.28	0.57	0.56	0.25	0.36	0.51	0.27	0.39	0.42	0.20	-0.03	

ANNEX IV

POLISH LOCAL GOVERNMENT IN INTERNATIONAL PERSPECTIVE

1.   The assessment of Poland's local finances in the interantional, comparative perspective, can be tentative at best. A relatively short time that has elapsed since local governments were established does not allow to draw firm conclusions as to their role in general government and in the provision of public services. After operating under a transitory financial framework in 1990, a new system of local government finances, marking a departure from the past, was introduced for 1991. While a number of its facets is going to be modified or removed, the local budget law for 1992 retains the core characteristics of the current system of local finance. Our analysis is restricted to data projected for 1991, although occassionally references to earlier developments will be made.

2.   The group used for comparative analysis is restricted to European unitary countries. Although some powerful political groups in Poland argue in favor of federalism, there are no seperate regional governments with well defined functions as well as clear financial powers and responsibilities.[1] Poland's general government consists of three major levels: central government, voivodhsips, and local governments. Voivodships (departments) have limited autonomy: major personnel decisions are in discretion of a central government, and most of their funding comes directly from the state budget. They do not have the power to raise revenue from sources under their control. Local governments, run by elected officials, exercize independent competence in local matters that are left to their jurisdiction. As can be seen in Table 1, the structure of general government in Poland does not have any unique traits. The last column containing data on the average population per local government should be treated with caution because of substantial dispersion in individual countries. It is nonetheless interesting to note that the average for Poland is not significantly different than in three other countries of our sample.

Table 1:   Structure of General Government in European Unitary Countries

Country	Supernational	Central govern.	Regions	Departments	Local	Average Size of Localities (in '000)
Belgium	1	1	3(C)	3(R)	589	17
Denmark	1	1		14	275	18.5
France	1	1	22	96	36,000	1.6
Hungary	0	1	8	20	3,100	3.5
Netherlands	1	1	-	12(P)	714	20.7
Poland	0	1	-	49	2,417	15.9
United Kingdom	1	1	9(R)*	54	540	105.9

R: Regions; C: Communities; P: Provinces
* includes Scotland

Sources: Jeffrey Owens, Local Government Taxation, Institute of Revenues, Rating and Valuation, Paris, 1991, and Powierzchnia i ludnosc w przekroju terytorialnym, Central Statistical Office, Warsaw 1991

---

[1] The difference between unitary and federalist arrangements is that while regional authorities may enjoy a significant degree of operating independence in unitary countries, this is not constitutionally guaranteed. This is the result of administrative decentralization.

3.   The extent of a government's involvement in providing public services
can be proxied by the share of its expenditure in GDP. Measured by this stick,
the role of central government in Poland is rather limited. Given the size of
the state-owned sector and a contraction of GDP in 1990 and 1991, it is rather
surprising that the portion of GDP distributed through the general government
in Poland is significantly lower than in other unitary countries (see Table
2). The share projected for 1991 is at the level of shares observed in the
west before the pervasive expansion of the public sector that occurred in the
1970s and 1980s. For instance, the share amounted to 35 percent in France in
1960, 32 percent in England, and 31 percent in Sweden.[2] It is interesting to
note that the Polish pattern also is substantially different from the
Hungarian pattern, despite similar legacies of the administrative,
centralized, economic system. This relatively low level of a general
government's involvement in a provision of public goods is not the result of
policy measures introduced after the collapse of the communist regime, as the
government's expenditure shrank in the second half of the 1980s. The share
declined from 39 percent in 1985 to 29 percent in 1989: the average for this
period was 35 percent.[3]

Table 2:   General Government Expenditure (consolidated) as percentate of GDP
            in Selected European Unitary Countries in 1987

Country	Percentage
Belgium	55.2
Denmark	57.6
France	49.1
Hungary	63.5
Netherlands	59.9
Poland	36.6
United Kingdom	43.2
Memo:	
Poland*	35.6

* Planned in 1991

4.   The relative importance of the local government level is not
significant. While the share of consolidated general government's expenditure
in GDP is lower, the degree of centralization--as measured by the shares of
each level of government in total expenditure (excluding intragovernmental
transfers)--seems to be relatively high. As can be seen in Table 3, a little
more than one tenth of expenditure is conducted at a local level. Poland
together with Belgium have the most centralized pattern of public spending;
they both fall well below the average (77%). The provision of public services
also is much more centralized than in Hungary.

---

[2] See World Development Report 1988, p. 44, Table 2.1.

[3] Calculated from data in Rocznik Statystyczny (Statistical yearbook),
Glowny Urzad Statystyczny, Warszawa 1990.

Table 3:   Expenditure of Each Level of Government in Selected Unitary
              Countries in 1988 (expressed as percentage of total expenditure)

Country	Central	Local
Belgium	88.5	11.5
Denmark	54.9	45.1
France	82.9	17.1
Netherlands	76.3	23.7
United Kingdom	75.4	24.6
Memo: Poland	88.3	11.7
(as planned for 1991)		

It is noteworthy that the share of the intermediate level, i.e., voivodships,
in general government expenditure was projected for 1991 at 14.8 percent, and
the central government's share at 73.5 percent.

5.   The relatively high degree of centralization of government in Poland is
reflected in a low share of local governments in tax revenue. Table 4 provides
an overview of the attribution of taxes (excluding social security) to
different levels of government in selected, unitary countries. The average
share of the local level of 12.4 (standard deviation - 9.3) percent is
significantly higher than the share to be accrued to local governments in
Poland in 1991. Shared taxes over which beneficiaries have no influence
account for about 60 percent of tax revenues of the local level of government.

Table 4:   Tax Revenues for the Main Local Taxes as Percentage of Total Tax
              Revenues of Local Governments in Selected Countries

Country	PIT	CIT	Wage Tax	Property Tax	Other
Belgium	62.3	14.5	-	-	23.2
Denmark	90.4	1.7	-	7.8	0.1
France	14.7	-	4.2	25.4	55.7
Netherlands	-	-	-	73.5	26.5
United Kingdom	-	-	-	100.0	-
Spain	15.0	3.7	-	0.6	80.7
Memo: Poland planned for 1991	-	25.0	-	24.0	51.0

Source: IMF statistics and Poland's Budget Act for 1991

6.   Despite major changes in the economic system, Poland's tax revenue
structure remains typical for a command economy. Among the countries for which
information is presented in Table 5, Poland stands out on two counts.

Table 5: Receipts from main taxes as percentage of GDP in current prices

Unitary Countries	Total tax	PIT *	CIT **	Other taxes	Consumption tax ***
Belgium	45.1	14.4	3.1	17.2	10.4
Denmark	58.1	26.6	2.3	6.7	16.5
France	44.4	5.4	2.3	24.0	12.7
Netherlands	48.2	9.9	3.5	23.4	11.4
United Kingdom	37.3	9.9	3.6	24.8	9.6
Spain	32.8	7.1	2.1	23.6	
Memo: Poland planned for 1991	30.2	0.6	17.1 ***	12.5	8.8

*   Personal income tax
**   Corporate income tax
*** Including dividend/levy on capital assets of SOEs (excluding - 14.4%)

First, the State Owned Sector is a major source of revenue. CIT's share in GDP (17.1%) by far is the largest in the sample, albeit total tax revenue as a share of GDP is the lowest. Second, receipts from PIT (with a very limited base) are estimated (0.6% of GDP) to account for only a tiny fraction of the lowest share (Spain--7.1%[4]) among countries presented in Table 5. This clearly is a transitional revenue structure.

---

[4] Note that Spain's ratio of total tax revenue to GDP of 32.3 percent is the closest to the Polish one (30.2%).

ANNEX V

INTERGOVERNMENTAL DISTRIBUTION OF SERVICE DELIVERY RESPONSIBILITIES

1.   This Annex provides a summary of the distribution of service delivery responsibilities for those services mentioned in the Local Self-Government Act as being of local responsibility. This summary is based on the December 1991 mission's visits to gminas and Voivodship offices.

Urban Transport

2.   Policy-making and Planning Process. Voivoidships are responsible for intergmina urban transport. Cities take care of urban transport within their boundaries. Public enterprises either owned by gminas or voivoidships generally provide the service. There is no systematic planning process made. This situation leads to inefficiencies in transport operation and difficulties arise particularly in large urban areas like Katowice. In fact, without general urban transport planning in a metropolitan area, each city enterprise operates independently from its neighbors, leading to a bad service for users. The lack of planning also applies to vehicles' maintenance which is poor.

3.   Finance. Urban transport is heavily subsidized. There is no relation made between operational costs and tariffs. Formerly owned by voivoidships, assets are being transferred to gminas without the equivalent funding. Public transport enterprises generally do not separate operation and maintenance costs from capital expenditures. Furthermore, there is no reserve for the equipment renewal, which is a major issue for the next coming years.

4.   Other Findings. The following table describes the urban transport key elements in Katowice, Radom and Kielce. The figures related to the number of employees include personnel involved in matters not related to the operation itself (housing, resorts, etc.). Up to 20% of personnel is in this situation.

Table 1. Urban Transport Indicators of Selected Gminas (1991)

	Katowice	Kielce	Radom
Passenger/year	1,000,000,000	90,000,000	72,000,000
Employees	10,472	1,009	889
Vehicles - Trams - Trolleys - Buses - Total	500 23 1,500 2,023	- - 258 258	 259 259
Lines - Total - KM	454 8,415	47 535	39 450
Tariff (zl)/Trip	2,000	1,600-3,400	1,200
Cost (zl)/Trip	3,000	-	1,700
Subsidy (zl)/Trip	1,000	-	500

Roads

5.   Policy-making and Planning Process. There are three categories of roads
in Poland. These roads categories are related to the authority responsible
for their construction and maintenance: national, voivoidship, local.
Generally, the voivoidships are responsible for both national and voivoidship
roads. There is a lack of coordination between the voivoidships and gminas
for the maintenance and snow removal of roads. Therefore, gminas often must
take care of national and voivoidship roads, in spite the fact this is not
their responsibility.

6.   Finance. Theoretically, each level of government must finance the
construction and maintenance of its own roads. In practice, most of the time
gminas must pay even for national and voivoidship roads. It is obvious that
upper levels of government are neglecting their responsibilities, leaving
gminas with insufficient funding and technical resources to perform this task.

Environment

7.   Policy-making and Planning Process. The Ministry of Environment is
responsible for all policy-making and planning matters. These policies are
operated by each voivoidship. Their main tasks are: water control and water
protection, air protection, natural resources and plants protection. They
also perform regular inspection of factories and plants to assure compliance
with environmental standards.

8.   Finance. Voivoidships' activities are financed through an "extra-
budgetary" fund. This special fund is self-financed by user charges, fees and
fines collected by the voivoidship mainly from industrial enterprises.
"Extra-budgetary" funds are largely insufficient to finance all investments
that should be done to restore the quality of grounds, air, and water. For
instance, the "extra-budgetary" funds of Katowice voivoidship is 4.44 Billion
zl in 1991 and the minimum needs would be five times greater.

Land Management and Regulation

9.   Policy-making and Planning Process. In its broader sense, spatial
planning policies are under the responsibility of the central government.
However, land use planning has been delegated to gminas which are subject to
voivoidships' control for final approval of zoning plans. Voivoidships are
responsible for geodesy and cadastre. Most important gminas have their own
cadastre office based on agreements with the voivoidship.

10.   Finance. Each level of government must finance its allocated
responsibility. Geodesy is financed through and "Extra budgetary" fund
similar to the one for Environment. This special fund is self-financed
through fees and development charges.

11.   More information is presented in Annex VII entitled "Local Land
Management and Regulation."

Housing

12.   Policy-making and Planning Process. The central government is responsible for the general Housing Policy and there are several legal rules and ordinances related to that area. The new Housing Act has not been adopted yet.

13.   The general Housing Policy stipulates that in the future, the citizens will individually decide the selection of investing and realization form of housing they wish. The system of bank credits for housing will be remodeled and will operate on a free market economy basis.

14.   Housing ownership is regulated by various legal frameworks: private, cooperative, municipal, and state owned properties. The existing stock amounts to about 11.2 M. flats (7.3 M. in cities and towns) of which:

    -4.6 M. are one-family house.

    -2.8 M. are of housing cooperative type.

    -2.1 M. are of municipal type.

    -1.1 M. are owned by enterprises and institutions.

    -0.6 M. is a private ownership of multi-family houses.

15.   State-owned housing enterprises are being transferred to gminas, which have undertaken a privatization process of their stock.

16.   Finance. Public housing is heavily subsidized all over the country. The central government controls the rent values and energy tariffs. For instance, rent values range from 800 to 1600 zl./square meter, depending on the quality of flats. Generally, the rents cover only a part of operating costs: cleaning, garbage collection, cold water, and sewage. Maintenance, hot water and heating are subsidized. Subsidies range from 40% to 60% of total housing operating costs in the visited gminas.

17.   Other Findings. The quality of the existing stock of flats is poor. In total, about 1.3 M. flats are in use for a period of over 70 years, in Poland. The share of buildings erected before 1945 amounts to 35%. In towns, 21% of flats have no bathroom, 30% no central heating and 17% no lavatories with running water. In the country, as much as 43% of houses do not have a water supply system. Over 1 M. flats are requiring urgent repairs and modernization.

Heating and Hot Water

18.   Policy-making and Planning Process. No general policy related to heating and hot water supply has been adopted. Only technical regulations have been issued by the Ministry of Physical Planning and Construction. Therefore, the planning process is weak, not to say inexistent.

19.   Voivoidships and gminas share the responsibility for heating enterprises. Heating enterprises are independent from one gmina to another. Cities and towns may have more than one enterprises, according to the size and type of heating plants.

20.   The transfer of voivoidships' heating enterprises to gminas was scheduled to be completed by end-1991. However, many gminas were not really interested in receiving these assets that are generally in poor condition.

21.   Finance. Communal heating and hot water enterprises are heavily subsidized by voivoidships. The central government subsidizes cooperatives and other types of heating enterprises.

22.   Flats are not equipped with meters. Thus, it is not easily possible to introduce user charges for hot water, other than by flat rates.

23.   Finally, heating enterprises' accounting systems do not make the distinction between operating and capital costs.

Water Supply and Sanitation

24.   Policy-making and Planning Process. There is no general policy concerning water supply and sanitation other than one technical regulation issued by the Ministry of Physical Planning and Construction

25.   Voivoidships are responsible for water supply and sanitation enterprises. These enterprises will be transferred to gminas in 1992. Where an enterprise provides the service to more than one gmina, the transfer will be made to an association of all interested gminas. Therefore, gminas will take over the planning of the network, as well as its maintenance.

26.   Finance. Water supply enterprises are self-financing their operating and maintenance costs but do not take into account the amortization of capital costs. Tariffs cover expenses related to both water supply and sanitation operations. These tariffs are based on a square meter basis of buildings. This is rather an inappropriate approach of tariffing since it does not take into account the individual consumption of each flat. In the visited voivoidships, tariffs range as follows:

Houses:	1,300 - 1,700 zl/m2
Institutions:	1,900 - 3,000 zl/m2
Industries:	6,000 - 6,500 zl/m2

27.   Other Findings. Usually water is drawn from surface water intakes (sometimes far away from consumption places), or from artesian wells. Generally, water supplied to cities is of a low quality.

28.   The sewage system in towns is fairly well developed, as against the sewage-treatment system being often insufficient. Rural localities are poorly sewered.

29.   The following table gives the percentage of population served by piped sewage and piped water supply in five visited cities.

Table 2.   Percentage of Population Served by Sewage and Water Supply
              Selected Gminas (1991)

	Water Supply	Sewage
Katowice	100%	80%
Kielce	90%	80%
Radom	90%	80%
Szydlowiec	95%	60%
Zabrze	100%	80%

Waste Disposal

30.   Policy-making and Planning Process.   There is no general policy regarding solid waste management in Poland.   There is no law or regulation related to the collection and disposal of solid waste, nor to any tariffing policy.   So far, voivoidships were responsible for disposal sites location and gminas for the collection of solid waste.   The best way to describe this area is a "free for all".   In fact, there is no obligation for anybody to use local waste collection enterprises.   The only obligation is to dispose solid waste at public garbage disposal sites on an individual basis or through any private or public garbage collection enterprise.

31.   Finance.   All visited solid waste management enterprises were self-financing their operation and even making "profits".   Their accounting system does not take into account capital costs which means that the claimed profitable operation is questionable.   Garbage collection tariffs range widely from one gmina to another (15,000 - 40,000 zl per cubic meter) depending on the number and category (residential, commercial, industrial) of customers. Most of gminas' enterprises are also responsible for streets and parks cleaning. Thus, there might be some hidden subsidies.

32.   Table 3 provides an overview of responsibility assignments.

Table 3.   Intergovernmental Distribution of Responsibilities

Key Sectors	Central Government Ministries						Voivodships						Local Governments					
	Policy & Norms	Planning & Design	Evaluation & Design	Execution Invest	Execution O&M	Financing	Policy & Norms	Planning & Design	Evaluation & Design	Execution Invest	Execution O&M	Financing	Policy & Norms	Planning & Design	Evaluation & Design	Execution Invest	Execution O&M	Financing
Public Housing	P											S	S	P	P	P	P	P
Heating & Hot Water	S					S		P	P	P	P	P	S	P	P	P	P	P
Waste Disposal							S											
Water Supply & Sanitation	S						S	P	P	P	P	P		P	P	P	P	
Roads	P	S	S	S	S	P	S	P	P	P	P	P	S	P	P	P	P	P
Urban Transport					S	S							P	P	P	P	P	P
Environment	P						S	P	P	P	P	P	P					
Land Use Planning	P							P	P	S	S	P	P	P	S	P	P	S
Geodesy & Cadastre	P						P	P	P	P	P	P	S	S	S	S	S	S

P = Primary Responsibility
S = Secondary Responsibility

As per December 1991

ANNEX VI

PLANNING AND MANAGEMENT OF LOCAL GOVERNMENT INFRASTRUCTURE

A. Background

1.   Local governments (gminas) are charged with the responsibility, *inter alia*, of providing, directly or indirectly, local public utilities and services including garbage, water, sewerage, transport, municipal housing and heating. Not all gminas will provide services in all sectors. For example, small gminas within the area of influence of large cities or conurbations may not provide transport; similarly small gminas may not provide water supply if individual well-supplies are adequate. However, whatever services are provided, it is axiomatic that those services should be provided in the most cost-effective manner possible although gminas do not have an entirely free hand in the administration of services (e.g., heating charge are centrally controlled). Nevertheless, under the Local Self Government Act, gminas are permitted considerable flexibility in the manner in which services are provided. Services may be provided directly by gmina enterprises or, gminas may create the climate whereby the private sector manages or provides services to meet performance standards defined and monitored by local governments. Whichever direction is taken by local governments, good planning for the provision, operation and maintenance of services is essential.

2.   Currently, gminas generally face massive problems in the supply of public utility services; these are often inadequate and of poor standard and, even where services exist, they often require expansion, modernization and maintenance. The Bank missions of June 1991 and December 1991 visited a wide range of gminas, including some within large conurbations, and identified the nature of the problems encountered in the provision of public utilities. Gminas visited by the Bank missions are shown in Table 1.

B. Technical Issues

3.   Based on discussions with elected representatives and officials, the main technical and operational problems[1] faced by gminas in the provision of services can be summarized as:

(a)   gminas have "inherited" (or will inherit) on-going projects commenced prior to 1990 by the voivodships and federal agencies. Gminas had little role in planning or selecting these projects and, now face problems arising from (i) lack of completeness; many of the projects have been

---

[1] The provision of public services is not concerned with technical and operational aspects in isolation; inter-actions with financial (eg levels of available resources) and other factors (eg freedom to determine levels of service and prices) of course also are important.

Table 1. Gminas visited during June and December 1991 missions

GMINA	POPULATION
Lubomia	8,000
Jablonna	8,000
Siewearz	13,000
Garwolin	16,000
Szudlowiec	23,500
Zabrze	200,000
Kielce	240,000
Radom	250,000
Lublin	360,000
Katowice	366,000
Warsaw	1,650,000

under construction for long periods but resources do not exit for their
completion, (ii) projects which are inappropriate in scale and capacity as a
result of a central planning system which was unable to respond to local needs
and problems and, (iii) poor quality of construction or equipment;

(b)   backlog and deficiencies in many services. Clearly the nature and
        severity of problems vary by gmina size. For example, small gminas have
        no urban transport problems, little centralized heating and,
        environmental problems are less pressing than in large gminas. However,
        medium and large gminas suffer to varying degrees from problems in all
        sectors and lack of sewerage treatment, inefficient heating networks,
        lack of coverage of garbage collection services and diminishing disposal
        sites are common themes; and

(c)   inexperienced institutions to plan, contract, manage, operate and
        maintain public utility services. Particular lack of experience was
        identified in such areas:

        *   strategic city planning in medium and larger gminas (where it is
                vital);
        *   investment planning;
        *   consideration of technical and economic alternatives;
        *   application of competitive contract procedures;
        *   application of full accounting principles to enterprises
                (particularly important where gmina enterprises will continue);
        *   management information systems and utilization of data; and
        *   planned maintenance and maintenance systems.

4.   The lack of institutional capacity and experience is regarded as a key issue in the efficient provision of public utility services and in the reform of local government in Poland. To improve delivery of public utilities, it is essential that local governments are able to plan, operate, manage and maintain services in an efficient manner and thus, it is with institutional experience and problems that the remainder of this Annex is concerned.

Policy Making and Planning

5.   There is not a lack of technical urban engineering competence in Poland. However, "planning" functions are less well developed. Formerly, gmina planning responsibilities were strictly limited; planning often comprised only a formulated response to central government or voivodship directives rather than systematic identification of city needs and an objective analyses of solutions leading to policy decisions.

6.   Given this history, it is difficult to assess the capabilities of the gminas as planning institutions since (i) they have had little opportunity to display initiative and decision making and, (ii) there is an apparent lack of familiarity with analytical procedures and critical approach to evaluation. Particular areas of planning where city visits have demonstrated shortcomings are summarized in the following sections.

7.   Strategic Planning Strategic city planning is the procedure whereby resources (land, facilities) and services (water, transport, sewerage etc) are planned and developed to provide optimum levels of service under defined policy and financial constraints. The planning procedure involves definition of present and future problems, development and evaluation of alternative strategies, and selection and justification of a preferred strategy. In the past, strategic planning was closely and centrally controlled and gminas had little influence on its direction. Gminas will now have to assume a greater planning role. Appropriate skills and approaches are not universally available, especially in the smaller gminas, and must be built-up. Particular problems and actions which need urgent consideration are:

(a)   the quantified identification of existing and potential problems and deficiencies in the provision of services such that inter-sectoral priorities can be established and actions determined before needs reach crisis point; and

(b)   a need to re-consider planning guidelines and norms (eg housing densities, accessibility to transport, parking standards etc) which respond more closely to local needs. City land-use planning can have a large impact on the costs of provision of utilities and services; it is evident that, for example in some gminas, densification of housing rather than spatial expansion, which is often the policy in Poland, could reduce the extent and thus the costs of provision of main services (water, communal heating, drainage, transport etc).

8.   Policy Planning - Privatization Implications.   "Privatization" of public
entities is a major plank in gminas approach to the provision of services.
Most gminas are considering privatization of at least some public utilities
and services. However, due to the lack of experience in managing contracts,
it is not evident that privatization conditions are being adequately defined
to ensure that the services meet gmina objectives. It will be necessary for
gminas to establish the privatization framework which will specify criteria
such as (i) the level of service required from the privatized services, (ii)
the controls on quality which will be exercised by gminas, (iii) the gmina
agency which will monitor and control service levels, (iv) the extent (if any)
to which gminas wish to control tariffs and charges, and (v) the form of
contract with private sector operators (form of bidding, duration of contract,
obligations, penalties etc). There is no evidence that gminas have yet begun
to consider the full implications of managing privatized services.

Operational Practices

9.   In addition to planning, gminas will assume greatly increased
responsibilities for the day-to-day delivery or management of some services
and infrastructure. However, gminas are currently operationally weak and
particular problem areas include:

(a)   Competitive contract procedures Gminas, particularly the smaller gminas,
      have not had exposure to competitive contract procedures.   The
      inherited on-going infrastructure and public utility projects generally
      had contractors in place. For completion of works, new or revised
      contracts have often been negotiated but competitive bidding has not
      taken place and new contractors or suppliers have been engaged without
      conventional contracts or bidding procedures, without defined
      performance or quality criteria and without procedures to control or
      monitor the works or services provided. The current trend appears to be
      for firms or suppliers to make "offers" to gminas and for gminas to
      negotiate a price. However, if gminas are to get the type of works or
      services they require at competitive prices coupled with accountability
      for quality and performance, then improved contract procedures will have
      to be defined and applied;

(b)   Operational practices. Many gminas consider that services should be
      "privatized" wherever possible. However, it appears that gminas
      understand that a "privatized" enterprise is a self accounting unit
      which may still be owned by a gmina. However, privatization may not be
      appropriate in all cases and in some cases, gminas may retain full
      operational control. In the short term, both types of enterprise are
      likely to retain their old operational practices (eg the flat fare
      system on the buses, the "on-demand" refuse collection system, the
      allocation of workers to duties, etc). In the interests of efficiency,
      it is desirable for gminas to review the operational practices of the
      enterprises over which they have control, and, cause to be reviewed the
      operational practices of the "privatized" enterprises. The review
      should lead to a critical evaluation of practices with the aim of
      increasing efficiency and responsiveness;

(c) <u>Management information systems</u>. Good planning, operation, management, maintenance and investment decisions require information as their bases. Particularly in the larger cities, much data (inventories, operational data etc) exist and are periodically up-dated. However, it appears that much of the data are historic in format. It is not clear that the data are used or provide the type of information on costs, on performance, on usage, etc which are necessary to assess efficiency of services and to establish maintenance, repair or replacement programs. Furthermore, it is not clear that the data are channeled to units with responsibility for budgetary control or decisions. Improved information systems will be an important element in developing efficient planning and operation of gmina public services;

(d) <u>Maintenance</u>. Preventive and routine maintenance of infrastructure is not undertaken as a separate task by most gminas. The current approach appears to be to repair and/or replace when problems arise. Some utilities and infrastructure already require extensive replacement due to their poor state and lack of past maintenance (particularly heating distribution systems or in special cases such as water supply in Katowice which is subject to damage by mining subsidence). Thus, there is a present emphasis on "deferred" repair/rehabilitation and this is probably the only course. Nevertheless, there is a danger that unless greater attention is paid to developing a planned maintenance approach, future problems will be even greater and repairs/rehabilitation now being undertaken will not realize their full potential.

Expenditure Planning and Implementation

10.   Gmina investment planning is at an early stage of development and will evolve and improve. At the moment, gminas appear to adopt a one-year investment planning approach and little distinction is made between capital investment costs, operation costs and maintenance costs. It is accepted that future revenues, and consequently investments, are difficult to define. However, there is a need (i) to make a distinction between capital investment planning and re-current cost budgeting and, (ii) to move multi-year investment planning. Not least, the latter is essential to demonstrate, and to allow gminas to make provision for, the full cost implications on subsequent years' budgets of commencing, but not completing in one year, high cost projects.

11.   Investment planning for services cannot be separated from technical and economic evaluation of alternatives either at the strategic planning, or at the project, levels. Increasingly, gminas will be responsible for new rather than on-going or inherited projects as the back-log of old projects is cleared and new strategic directions are established. It will be necessary for gminas to ensure that new projects and services are provided in the most cost effective manner. Consideration and comparative evaluation of technical alternatives is not current, common practice. In the future, it will be necessary for gminas:

(a)   to consider alternative technical solutions to determine the most cost-effective solutions;

(b)   to consider phasing of alternatives to avoid over-dimensioned projects
        and conserve scarce resources;

(c)   to include full costs (particularly depreciation which is totally absent
        from any analyses) in the analyses of projects; and

(d)   to evaluate the financial and economic return of alternatives.

12.   Such analyses are clearly necessary for large projects, such as the
Warsaw metro, Warsaw and Katowice solid waste composting plants, new sewage
treatment works in most larger gminas etc. However, even in smaller gminas,
technical and economic evaluations are essential; the impacts of
infrastructure investment on gmina budgets are proportionally high regardless
of gmina size and the need to ensure "value for money" is equally important to
small, as well as to large, gminas.

C. Financial Planning, Budgeting and Reporting

Executive Level and Organization

13.   Political and Managerial Relationships. The relationship between local
elected people and senior managers of gminas is operating fairly well. Each
elected council appoints a manager in charge of the day to day operation of
the gmina. The manager is reporting directly to the mayor and the council.
Each gmina has also set an executive board made of a few members of the
council. All visited gminas have established a set of committees made of
elected representatives and appropriate operating managers. Each committee is
responsible for a specific area: finance, public works, education, health,
culture, transport, etc. All major decisions in each assigned area must be
submitted to the appropriate committee, then approved by the council.

14.   Organization. In spite the fact that many new responsibilities have
recently been assigned to gminas, they already have an understanding about the
way these tasks must be split between different departments. Each gmina has
its own organizational chart. Operational responsibilities are properly
established, as well as functional ones. The number of employees per 1000
inhabitants is much lower for cities than for towns and villages. The
rationale for such a situation is that in larger cities, economies of scale
occur; in addition, figures related to smaller towns include the staff for
communal enterprises. The staff/population ratios of Table 2 indicate
potentially great improvement in the cost effectiveness of providing some
local infrastructure and services on a regional basis, through associations of
gminas.

Table 2. Number of Employees of Selected Gminas (1991)

Gmina	Staff	Population	Staff/1000 inha.
Katowice	480	366,000	2.1
Radom	300	250,000	3.3
Zabrze	268	205,000	3.7
Kielce	200	215,000	5.0
Siewierz	40	13,050	25.0
Maslow	25	8,020	40.0
Lubomia	21	7,600	47.6

Asset Management

15.   Business Activities. Most of the visited gminas wish to expand their entrepreneurial activities to the detriment of their real business: provision of public services to citizens. The main reason for this behavior is to get additional source of revenues. Real estate development and housing seem to be the most attractive area of intended business. A few gminas even wish to acquire and operate enterprises involved in the production of private goods: food, building construction, furniture, etc.

16.   Further investigations would probably demonstrate a country-wide trend for most of the local governments to do so. This is another clear indication that local governments still need to be monitored by some central coordination unit. This is also an indication that local governments need to expand their own taxation fields.

17.   These entrepreneurial activities are inconsistent with the privatization drive. They are an impediment to true decentralization and to strengthening of the private sector. Therefore, clear rules should be set by the central government to ensure that local governments will focus on their primary tasks. An informal rule is already in force in Katowice voivoidship stating that the only state enterprises to be transferred to gminas must be related to their assigned responsibilities. This rule could be expanded throughout the country.

18.   Communalization and Asset Disposition. The process of transferring state property to gminas should be linked to a better local discipline and an appropriate asset disposition policy. To compensate their inadequate tax yields, local governments are using proceeds from asset sales to finance current operations. Furthermore, in many cases, asset sales are made at very low prices following a weak tendering process. Thus, where assets are to be sold, gminas should carefully assess their value. They should undertake sales through a disciplined and time-phased program enabling them to maximize net revenues.

19.   It is obvious that as long as the central government will control prices and rents in the real estate area (for instance in housing) the market will not perform as it should. Market prices will be better reached from a medium to long term period during which central interventions will decrease. Thus, gminas should refrain to dispose assets that are not exposed to a free market economy.

20.   An immediate rule should be set to use proceeds from asset sales only to finance new local investments. Among all visited gminas, only Krakow already set such a rule.

21.   Management Reform. Gminas must resist the temptation of staffing new technical positions in their organization in order to take care of newly transferred enterprises. They have an opportunity to act as asset managers. Their primary concern should be to appoint a competent board of directors and a qualified manager for each state enterprise that they will acquire. An effective approach may be to contract out the management of some of their enterprises to the private sector. An example of such practices is water supply and sanitation management in France. Joint ventures could also be developed in order to acquire the foreign knowledge in some specific areas. In these cases, however, the capacity to enter into contractual agreements must be strengthened (see Section D below).

Expenditures Planning and Budgeting

22.   Budgetary Process. The budget formulation and approval process could be improved. Different kinds of budgets should be implemented according to the nature of operations: current expenditures, investments, cash flow movements, additional budgets for unforeseen expenditures. The budget cycle should include clear steps for each of the three parts: planning, approval and execution.

23.   The practice of budget planning based heavily on the allocations of previous years should be replaced with resource envelops that permit changes according to the reshuffle of priorities. Consolidation of the budgets of public enterprises into the financial statements of the gminas also should be considered.

24.   Accounting and Auditing. The codification system, as well as the auditing and analysis of results, should be improved. The detailed codification needs clarification especially for two major items covering "Other revenues" and "Other expenditures". It seems that too many details exist for a few parts of the codification meanwhile other parts are too vague. Current expenditures and investments must clearly be reported under separate accounts. Auditing must be performed more systematically and reports submitted to the executive level of management. Performance indicators must be developed and results made available for public consultations.

25.   Budget Execution.   A better control over revenues collection and expenditures authorization should be exercised. Revenue and expenditure levels need to be reviewed regularly to ensure that they conform to planned

budget. When variations occur, proper adjustments should be made to the budget and the managers should be advised accordingly.

26.   Financial Management Information System. Financial management should be standardized in every gmina and proper support provided by the central government to improve local financial management. Guidelines and manuals are already provided by the regional offices of the Ministry of Finance. Nevertheless, there is a lack of uniformity in applying those guidelines, and many local accounting systems are manual. Training courses should be made available and a computerization program should be undertaken. The target should be to develop rapidly a computerized Financial Management Information System.

27.   The Financial Management Information System would serve both central and local governments. At the local level, it would be a useful tool for both financial analysts and managers. Accurate financial information produced on a regular and timely basis would help managers to adjust their operations, and appropriate corrections could be made when required. At the central level, the system would provide comparable financial data, making the performance analysis of gminas easier. It would also provide the base on which to identify local needs for technical assistance for improved financial management . Finally, such a system would feed the central government with an essential input for national fiscal policy decisions.

D. Technical Assistance Program

28.   To enable gminas to fulfill their role in the efficient delivery and management of infrastructure and public utilities, technical assistance to them will be very important. A technical assistance program might be divided broadly into the following three categories.

29.   Category 1 - technical assistance on procedures. The objective of the technical assistance would be to provide assistance to gmina technical staff on the procedures necessary for the efficient management, operation and implementation of public utilities. Typical areas of activity may include:

    (a)   competitive contract preparation, administration, management and
           supervision ("procurement"):
    (b)   economic evaluation of projects:
    (c)   planning and design of maintenance programs;
    (d)   financial evaluation of projects;
    (e)   investment program preparation;
    (f)   management information systems and reporting;
    (g)   budgeting, financial reporting and audit systems;
    (h)   city land use and utility planning;
    (i)   procedures for evaluation of supplier credits, aid offers;
    (j)   pricing of services;
    (k)   placing public utilities as independently managed and financially
           autonomous entities, and expanded private sector participation.

30.   The technical assistance could comprise seminars, training courses, case studies, dissemination of technical literature, possibly short overseas secondments, etc. The technical assistance would be international in character - the aim is to familiarize gmina staff with procedures not necessarily applied in Poland - and may be funded by channelization of donor funds. The technical assistance may be delivered at two levels. At the national level, coordination could be provided by the Municipal Development Agency and the National Assembly of Local Self Governments, where the emphasis would be on the development of strategy, standards and procedures. At the gmina level, coordination could be provided by the respective Voivod's office, where the emphasis would be on the dissemination of information and the training of gmina staff in the application of the procedures. Preparation of training materials and delivery of training could be provided predominantly by the private sector.

31.   Category 2: technical assistance to small gminas. The objective of the technical assistance would be to improve the quality of technical decisions and procedures in small gminas (those without resources to employ full time specialized professional staff). In principle, the technical assistance would comprise the provision of Polish engineers to smaller gminas to act as their "municipal engineer". Engineers would provide technical services to a number of gminas on a part time basis; the intention would be for one engineer to serve a number of gminas in an area. Specialists could also be provided if necessary. The technical service could be organized and provided along the same lines as Category 1. The engineers providing the service could receive training in procedures from the Category 1 technical assistance. Funding may be possible through international donors, through own resources or through loans.

32.   Category 3: technical expertise for major projects. The objective of the technical assistance would be to assist gminas to make planning and investment decisions on large, complex projects and programs. The technical assistance would be in the form of studies probably by international consultants/agencies but with gmina staff participation/counterpart as a condition of execution of any study. Typical studies might be the Warsaw metro or refuse composting program and similar projects in other major cities. Possible funding sources would be international donors or other development funds.

ANNEX VII

LOCAL LAND MANAGEMENT AND REGULATION

Introduction

1. The purpose of this annex is to describe the existing situation regarding land management and list issues and options to strengthen the Polish institutional capacity in this area.

2. The main conclusion is that at all levels of government there are strong technical capacities for geodesy and mapping; however, the legal framework related to land use planning and property rights is no longer appropriate. Most property titles are not clear for private or public properties.

3. The observations included in this paper are subject to certain limitations. Most of the information was gathered during a mission that occurred from December 4 to December 20, 1991. Among other organizations, the Ministry of Physical Planning and Construction which is responsible for land management, was visited. Our survey was also complemented by field visits to three voivoidship offices and ten gmimas - four cities, four towns, two villages - all of them located in the Southwestern part of Poland.

Responsibilities

4. Spatial organization and local land use planning is one of the new responsibilities delegated to local governments according to the Local Self-Government Act of March 22, 1990. Before this law, all responsibilities regarding spatial organization were centrally performed. Voivoidships were entitled to implement decisions made by the central government and all local requests related to land development had to be approved by the voivoda.

5. All matters related to geodesy, cartography and cadastre are part of a different organization. This area is more technical and requires day to day interventions in order to maintain a permanently updated data base.

6. Geodesy and cadastre are under the responsibility of voivoidships which have delegated it to their regional offices - "rejons". Most cities and towns prefer to be responsible for their own cadastre office. In such situations, rejons may delegate their responsibility to local governments within a special agreement contract. These agreements stipulate that local governments must comply with standard guidelines for all cadastre works and they are funded by the voivoidship to perform those duties.

Rights to Real Property

7. In Poland, private ownership of land was allowed during the socialist era. Poland placed certain land under state ownership, including all of Warsaw, about 60% of other urban land, land occupied by state-enterprises, and about 20% of agricultural land.

8.   "Social ownership" (state, cooperatives and social organizations) was the highest category of ownership and was protected by the Constitution and the Civil and Criminal Codes. Typically, such property included means of production, including, for example, land, mineral resources and public utilities.

9.   Property used for personal consumption was individually owned and considered "personal property". This category could include one's dwelling house but not a rental house, which was considered a means of production.

10.   On December 29, 1989, the Polish Constitution was amended to eliminate the socialist property classification and instead treat all types of property equally in civil, administrative and criminal matters. This amendment implies full protection of private property.

Progress in Legislation and Regulatory Works

11.   A series of five regulations related to the Act on Changes in Land Use and Expropriation (passed in September 1990) has just been adopted. These regulations concern:

    (i)   Sales and all forms of lease of land belonging to gmimas or the State;

    (ii)   Transfer of ownership or lease rights onto individual plots and division of land into building plots;

    (iii) Methods of cost recovery of infrastructure investments, focusing on share of infrastructure costs in construction costs;

    (iv)   Penalty fees for non-compliance with the land-use plan; and

    (v)   Bidding procedures required in acquisition of municipal and State property.

12.   A new Spatial Planning Act has been presented to the Parliament but was not adopted in December 1991. The proposed legislation distinguishes two separate types of physical planning: (i) the governmental planning as the instrument of national or regional development policy; and (ii) the local planning as an instrument of land use policy.

13.   The governmental physical planning is an instrument designed to achieve two major targets: (i) environmental protection; and (ii) protection of civil rights of property owners against decisions taken by public authorities.

14.   The local physical planning is a new competence of local authorities giving them total control over land use, subject to one limitation: preliminary approval by the voivoidship before adoption by the gmina council.

Cadastre and Property Registration

15.   From a technical point of view, the cadastre is satisfactory all over Poland. Maps cover 100% of the Polish territory. These maps have a scale of 1:10,000; furthermore, 50% of the territory is covered by maps with scales of 1:5,000, 1:2,000, 1:1,000 and even 1:500 in certain areas more densely built.

16.   The cadastre has been permanently updated and is easy to maintain, in spite of the fact that it is manually managed almost everywhere. A few cities and regions have already started to computerize their mapping system.

17.   Each parcel of land is clearly identified by a number and the boundaries of each property are shown on all maps. Each property is associated to its owner. The occupant is identified when the legal ownership has not been established.

18.   Two sets of registry books are available: the occupancy registry book and the legal one. The occupancy registry book is a technical register kept by the cadastre office and the legal one is supervised by a judge.

Issues and Options

19.   Land Use Planning. The relation between government (central and local) planning is not clear and their targets are sometimes confused. For example, among other targets for local physical planning, one is the protection of public interests and another is the creation of advantageous conditions for activities undertaken by developers. Identification of clear and non conflicting objectives in the future Spatial Planning Act is essential.

20.   The proposed Spatial Planning Act is inconsistent with the Local Self Government Act of 1990. The Local Self-Government Act gives full autonomy to gmimas in the area of planning and land development, but the Spatial Planning Act presented to the Parliament provides many controls by the voivoidships over gmimas' responsibilities.

21.   There are also inconsistencies with the new Land Use and Expropriation Act regulations. For instance, in cases where a private owner wishes to subdivide land for housing, the final permission on development rests with the "rejon" and not with the gmimas.

22.   If all these inconsistencies were removed, it would simplify the approval processes in all areas (e.g., zoning, building permits, housing developments, etc.), and it would facilitate the transition towards a market economy.

23.   Reprivatization. Compensation for expropriated former owners is a major issue related to real property. The severity of the problem varies in importance in different parts of the country, according to the level of public ownership. Among other issues, how far back in time to go, whether to offer monetary or in-kind compensation and what form compensation procedures should take, are the most important. Unsettled claims on land make land sales difficult and stalls investment.

24.   Reprivatization is an area where technical assistance may be appropriate. Poland is in a position to learn from other post-socialist countries that have already moved ahead in this area.

25.   Communalization. The process of transferring state property to local governments has been initiated but is very slow. There are disputes between gmimas and state enterprises due to the awarding to the latter of their own grounds. Until the land is inventoried, disputes resolved and land properly registered, local governments cannot make legal transactions to sell communal property.

26.   Land Registration. From a legal point of view, Poland's registry system is in a state of disarray. Under socialism, the legal registration system was largely neglected and many individuals did not comply with registration requirements. Many transfers were not recorded, particularly for the land under state ownership. Since a well-functioning registration system is essential for any market economy, a rehabilitation program should be put in place to improve the current system. Among other things, a computerization program should be introduced.

Conclusion

27.   From a technical point of view, land management is well under control in Poland. All matters related to geodesy and the cadastre are well performed but the system needs to be computerized. Therefore, local governments have an appropriate basic tool for part of their responsibilities: land use planning, zoning and property taxation.

28.   The key issue remains the legal framework for both land use planning and property rights. Real property rights are particularly sensitive for the transition to a market economy. Unless clear titles can be obtained and an adequate land registration system can be put in place, new private investment will be deterred.

ANNEX VIII

REORGANIZATION OF THE LOCAL REVENUE STRUCTURE: AN AGENDA

1.   The purpose of this annex is to suggest an agenda aiming at the improvement of self-financing of local responsibilities. A reorganization of the local revenue structure in Poland could strengthen local autonomy and reduce dependance of gmimas on central transfer payments.

2.   The decentralization process underway in Poland seems to substantially increase responsibilities of local governments without giving them the equivalent financial resources required to perform these new tasks. The suggested agenda will focus on immediate actions that both central and local governments could take to increase local own-source revenues on a short and medium terms basis.

Rates setting

3.   The current local tax base is very limited mainly because all tax rates and fees are subject to maximum caps set by the Ministry of Finance. In spite of the fact that these caps are low, many gmimas do not even use the maximum taxation rates available. It is well known by gminas that if they were using their full tax base, block grants would be cut by the Ministry of Finance. Such a practice is a clear indication that the Ministry of Finance should calculate its grants on the basis that gmimas may use their full tax base.

4.   There is a contradiction between the autonomy principle stated in the Local Self Government Act and the fact that the Ministry of Finance keeps a tight control over user charges, real estate taxation rates and administrative fees. There should be a removal of upper caps on all these rates, starting immediately.

5.   There is a wide range of real estate tax rates according to the occupancy. These discrepancies might be justified by the owners' ability to pay, but seem to be inequitable for certain categories of owners whose share of the tax burden appears to be unfair. For example, the tax rate for houses is 690 zl per square meter, compared to 26,000 zl for commercial buildings. There is no economic justification for such a large discrepancy, where commercial property taxes may be passed on to consumers. One may also wonder why farm buildings are excluded. There is an urgent need to revise the rate structure related to real estate tax.

Tax Collection

6.   An in depth analysis of the revenue losses in each category of own source revenues should be undertaken. According to the information provided by Treasurers of visited gmimas, the average losses due to the collection process range from 5% to 10% of planned revenues (tax bills).

7.   The tax base is limited by insufficient checking of self-declared taxable properties. Each owner is requested to self-declare the area of his

taxable buildings. Self-declaration forms are sent to the gmimas on a yearly basis. The problem is that there is no spot check made on the premises. The accuracy of information relies on an historical data base which contains the physical information declared when the premises were built. There is no evidence of updated information for additions or modifications to the buildings. Therefore, an on-site check of self-declaration of taxable buildings should be made systematically.

8.   Another area of immediate concern should be the legal framework for the case of delinquents. The law defines the property owner as liable for the property tax. However, the process is slow, and because ownership titles are not always clear, gmimas often waste energy trying to seize properties for unpaid taxes.

User Charges

9.   The first major step towards the reorganization of the local revenue structure should be the implementation of tariff policies. Generally, when it is possible to measure the individual or household consumption levels of urban services (e.g., water supply and sanitation, heating, urban transport, garbage disposal, housing) user charges should be applied.

10.   Two principles of equity can be the base of a tariff policy. The first is the "benefit principle". Under this principle, those who receive direct benefits from a service pay for it through a consumer charge related to their level of consumption. The second one is known as the "ability-to-pay principle". Charges based on this principle are related to the financial capacity of citizens to pay for urban services. Low-income households are charged a lower rate per unit of service than higher income groups.

11.   User charges may stimulate economic efficiency. Where individuals are free to choose how much of a service they consume, charging enables the price mechanism to play an important role of allocating resources through: rationing demand, providing the incentive to avoid waste, providing signals to the supplier concerning the scale of production, and providing the resources to the supplier to increase supply. With no or low price charges for the consumption of a good or service, the allocation of resources will not be economically efficient.

Property Tax Rehabilitation Program

12.   Poland has a great potential to increase local own-source revenues from property taxes. Property taxes represented 6.3 Billion zl or 17% of total planned revenue for gmimas in 1991. This amount could easily be doubled over a short period of time. In fact, in countries where an effective property tax system is in place, revenues raised from this source can reach up to 75% of total local budgets.

13.   From a technical point of view, Poland already has the most important basic tool to rehabilitate its property tax system: a good cadastre and mapping system. The whole territory is well covered by maps. Gmimas have

their own fiscal cadastre and a register of all owners and/or occupants of each property. These maps and registers are up-to-date (see Annex VII).

14.   The existing property tax system based on rates per square meter of land and buildings needs reform. A property tax reform based on the market value of properties would decrease inequities. A review and reduction of actual exemptions would also improve the fairness of the system and increase revenues.

15.   The most important basic elements for initiating a property tax reform in Poland are political commitment and an adequate legal framework. A strong commitment would result from clear limitations on national fiscal transfers, and the broad understanding that local public goods are to be financed primarily with local taxes. Furthermore, a national framework including laws and regulations should be established to promote local policies for the tax base and rate structure. Central control over rates should be abolished or reduced as much as possible; local governments must decide by themselves the appropriate rates required to provide sufficient revenues to face their responsibilities.

16.   The development and implementation of a property tax rehabilitation program is a key area where technical assistance will be appropriate. The development to the legal framework and the administrative process, including assessment manuals, are particularly important: many western countries could support Poland in those areas. Training is also an important area in which international organizations are already involved.

17.   Most gminas visited are eager to exercise their autonomy in financing their responsibilities. Their major concern is to be penalized by a reduction of grants from the central government if they are successful with new local initiatives. It is essential to create an intergovernmental fiscal system in which local initiatives to improve local resource mobilization, in accordance with local willingness to pay for services, is not penalized.

18.   A key role of the proposed Municipal Development Agency would be to propose, and support implementation of, local responsibilities and financing authority consistent with the LSGA and macroeconomic policy.

Distributors of World Bank Publications

ARGENTINA
Carlos Hirsch, SRL
Galeria Guemes
Florida 165, 4th Floor-Ofc. 453/465
1333 Buenos Aires

AUSTRALIA, PAPUA NEW GUINEA,
FIJI, SOLOMON ISLANDS,
VANUATU, AND WESTERN SAMOA
D.A. Books & Journals
648 Whitehorse Road
Mitcham 3132
Victoria

AUSTRIA
Gerold and Co.
Graben 31
A-1011 Wien

BANGLADESH
Micro Industries Development
    Assistance Society (MIDAS)
House 5, Road 16
Dhanmondi R/Area
Dhaka 1209

    Branch offices:
    156, Nur Ahmed Sarak
    Chittagong 4000

    76, K.D.A. Avenue
    Kulna 9100

BELGIUM
Jean De Lannoy
Av. du Roi 202
1060 Brussels

CANADA
Le Diffuseur
C.P. 85, 1501B rue Ampère
Boucherville, Québec
J4B 5E6

CHINA
China Financial & Economic
    Publishing House
8, Da Fo Si Dong Jie
Beijing

COLOMBIA
Infoenlace Ltda.
Apartado Aereo 34270
Bogota D.E.

COTE D'IVOIRE
Centre d'Edition et de Diffusion
    Africaines (CEDA)
04 B.P. 541
Abidjan 04 Plateau

CYPRUS
Cyprus College Bookstore
6, Diogenes Street, Engomi
P.O. Box 2006
Nicosia

DENMARK
SamfundsLitteratur
Rosenoerns Allé 11
DK-1970 Frederiksberg C

DOMINICAN REPUBLIC
Editora Taller, C. por A.
Restauración e Isabel la Católica 309
Apartado de Correos 2190 Z-1
Santo Domingo

EGYPT, ARAB REPUBLIC OF
Al Ahram
Al Galaa Street
Cairo

The Middle East Observer
41, Sherif Street
Cairo

EL SALVADOR
Fusades
Alam Dr. Manuel Enrique Araujo #3530
Edificio SISA, ler. Piso
San Salvador 011

FINLAND
Akateeminen Kirjakauppa
P.O. Box 128
SF-00101 Helsinki 10

FRANCE
World Bank Publications
66, avenue d'Iéna
75116 Paris

GERMANY
UNO-Verlag
Poppelsdorfer Allee 55
D-5300 Bonn 1

GUATEMALA
Librerias Piedra Santa
5a. Calle 7-55
Zona 1
Guatemala City

HONG KONG, MACAO
Asia 2000 Ltd.
46-48 Wyndham Street
Winning Centre
2nd Floor
Central Hong Kong

INDIA
Allied Publishers Private Ltd.
751 Mount Road
Madras - 600 002

    Branch offices:
    15 J.N. Heredia Marg
    Ballard Estate
    Bombay - 400 038

    13/14 Asaf Ali Road
    New Delhi - 110 002

    17 Chittaranjan Avenue
    Calcutta - 700 072

    Jayadeva Hostel Building
    5th Main Road Gandhinagar
    Bangalore - 560 009

    3-5-1129 Kachiguda Cross Road
    Hyderabad - 500 027

    Prarthana Flats, 2nd Floor
    Near Thakore Baug, Navrangpura
    Ahmedabad - 380 009

    Patiala House
    16-A Ashok Marg
    Lucknow - 226 001

    Central Bazaar Road
    60 Bajaj Nagar
    Nagpur 440010

INDONESIA
Pt. Indira Limited
Jl. Sam Ratulangi 37
P.O. Box 181
Jakarta Pusat

ISRAEL
Yozmot Literature Ltd.
P.O. Box 56055
Tel Aviv 61560
Israel

ITALY
Licosa Commissionaria Sansoni SPA
Via Duca Di Calabria, 1/1
Casella Postale 552
50125 Firenze

JAPAN
Eastern Book Service
Hongo 3-Chome, Bunkyo-ku 113
Tokyo

KENYA
Africa Book Service (E.A.) Ltd.
Quaran House, Mfangano Street
P.O. Box 45245
Nairobi

KOREA, REPUBLIC OF
Pan Korea Book Corporation
P.O. Box 101, Kwangwhamun
Seoul

MALAYSIA
University of Malaya Cooperative
    Bookshop, Limited
P.O. Box 1127, Jalan Pantai Baru
59700 Kuala Lumpur

MEXICO
INFOTEC
Apartado Postal 22-860
14060 Tlalpan, Mexico D.F.

NETHERLANDS
De Lindeboom/InOr-Publikaties
P.O. Box 202
7480 AE Haaksbergen

NEW ZEALAND
EBSCO NZ Ltd.
Private Mail Bag 99914
New Market
Auckland

NIGERIA
University Press Limited
Three Crowns Building Jericho
Private Mail Bag 5095
Ibadan

NORWAY
Narvesen Information Center
Book Department
P.O. Box 6125 Etterstad
N-0602 Oslo 6

PAKISTAN
Mirza Book Agency
65, Shahrah-e-Quaid-e-Azam
P.O. Box No. 729
Lahore 54000

PERU
Editorial Desarrollo SA
Apartado 3824
Lima 1

PHILIPPINES
International Book Center
Fifth Floor, Filipinas Life Building
Ayala Avenue, Makati
Metro Manila

POLAND
ORPAN
Palac Kultury i Nauki
00-901 Warzawa

PORTUGAL
Livraria Portugal
Rua Do Carmo 70-74
1200 Lisbon

SAUDI ARABIA, QATAR
Jarir Book Store
P.O. Box 3196
Riyadh 11471

SINGAPORE, TAIWAN,
MYANMAR, BRUNEI
Information Publications
    Private, Ltd.
02-06 1st Fl., Pei-Fu Industrial
    Bldg.
24 New Industrial Road
Singapore 1953

SOUTH AFRICA, BOTSWANA
For single titles:
Oxford University Press
    Southern Africa
P.O. Box 1141
Cape Town 8000

For subscription orders:
International Subscription Service
P.O. Box 41095
Craighall
Johannesburg 2024

SPAIN
Mundi-Prensa Libros, S.A.
Castello 37
28001 Madrid

Librería Internacional AEDOS
Consell de Cent, 391
08009 Barcelona

SRI LANKA AND THE MALDIVES
Lake House Bookshop
P.O. Box 244
100, Sir Chittampalam A.
    Gardiner Mawatha
Colombo 2

SWEDEN
For single titles:
Fritzes Fackboksforetaget
Regeringsgatan 12, Box 16356
S-103 27 Stockholm

For subscription orders:
Wennergren-Williams AB
Box 30004
S-104 25 Stockholm

SWITZERLAND
For single titles:
Librairie Payot
1, rue de Bourg
CH 1002 Lausanne

For subscription orders:
Librairie Payot
Service des Abonnements
Case postale 3312
CH 1002 Lausanne

TANZANIA
Oxford University Press
P.O. Box 5299
Maktaba Road
Dar es Salaam

THAILAND
Central Department Store
306 Silom Road
Bangkok

TRINIDAD & TOBAGO, ANTIGUA
BARBUDA, BARBADOS,
DOMINICA, GRENADA, GUYANA,
JAMAICA, MONTSERRAT, ST.
KITTS & NEVIS, ST. LUCIA,
ST. VINCENT & GRENADINES
Systematics Studies Unit
#9 Watts Street
Curepe
Trinidad, West Indies

UNITED KINGDOM
Microinfo Ltd.
P.O. Box 3
Alton, Hampshire GU34 2PG
England

VENEZUELA
Libreria del Este
Aptdo. 60.337
Caracas 1060-A